The Art of Influencing

by

Karen Lawson, Ph.D.

Illustrations by
Jennifer Lane

KENDALL/HUNT PUBLISHING COMPANY
4050 Westmark Drive   Dubuque, Iowa 52002

To the two greatest influencers in my life - my husband

and my mother. Their love and support

have truly made a difference.

Table of Contents

Preface

Throughout my life I have been influenced by many people - family, friends, teachers, colleagues, bosses, and participants in my workshops. I have observed them and tried to determine why some were so successful in dealing with people, regardless of the situation. After much reflection, I concluded that the key to their success was their ability to understand and relate to people. It sounds simple, doesn't it? But when I tried to analyze just what it was they actually *did*, I discovered that it was much more complex than I thought. I also discovered that it was a skill, a talent, yes, even an art they had developed and cultivated over the years.

I concluded that there are certain basic principles and practices in all human interactions. Our success or failure in those interactions and our relationships, in general, has less to do with our power or position and more to do with how well we practice fundamental interpersonal skills.

I reflected on my own behavior and assessed the reasons for my effectiveness and ineffectiveness in both my personal and professional interactions over the years. In doing so, I realized how much I have changed over the past twenty years. I've changed, not by chance, but by design.

I'm not sure when my "wake-up" call came, but I do remember the process I followed to change my life. I began by deciding who I wanted to be. Then I looked at who I was and quickly concluded that the real and ideal were pretty far apart. I went through a painful process of self-discovery and self-analysis to identify the reasons why I was not as effective in my relationships - personal and professional - as I wanted to be and knew I could be. I then embarked on a plan of self-improvement that included seeking and receiving feedback from others, becoming more positive about life, in general, and consciously replacing old negative behaviors with new positive ways of interacting with others. It's been a long journey but a rewarding one.

I wanted to share some of my observations and insights, and I hope that some of my "lessons learned" may help others to become who they want to be. That desire to synthesize those lessons and share them with the world has resulted in this book.

As with any other endeavor, this book was not created without the help of several people. First, I would like to thank my editor, Loretta Riley, for her patience and support throughout this process and also Kathleen Gullick, who helped in the editing process.

In particular, I want to express my deepest appreciation to my husband, Bob Lawson, for all his help in making this dream a reality. I couldn't have done it without him. And as always, I thank my mother, Mildred Eells, for her encouragement and inspiration.

Introduction

The humblest individual exerts some influence, either good or evil, upon others.

Henry Ward Beecher

Every day, every one of us is influenced by someone, and in turn, we influence others. Some one or some thing influences us to buy a piece of merchandise, vote for a particular individual, watch a television program, complete a project, or select a restaurant. Today, more than ever before, the ability or power to be a compelling force on the thoughts, behaviors, or opinions of others is critical.

Importance of Influencing

In today's world, lines of authority are blurred as people work cross-functionally in teams. Structurally flat organizations require people to manage processes and projects that involve people over whom they have no formal authority such as project teams, process improvement teams, task forces, etc. With the elimination of the hierarchical structure, leaders are relying more on their ability to influence in order to get things done.

People who have little power are capable of exercising tremendous influence on people with whom they interact, regardless of position. The truly powerful individual is one who relates to and interacts well with people at all levels. He or she possesses effective interpersonal skills.

Even in families, the traditional hierarchical structure and approach doesn't work the way it used to. Successful parenting, for example, often relies on the parents' ability to influence rather than dictate a child's behavior. Today the spousal or "significant other" relationship is one of equality. Gone are the days of the male authority figure. Today's couples see themselves as partners. As with any partnership, the parties involved use influencing skills to create and maintain a harmonious, meaningful, and mutually satisfying relationship.

Your Personal Influencing Style

Before we can begin to master the art of influencing, we need to take a look at what influences us and why. I asked a number of people to share with me what behaviors in other people influence them. The overwhelming response was "someone showing a genuine interest in me" by maintaining good eye contact, actively listening, asking open-ended questions, and giving a response that is directly related to what the person just said. People surveyed also mentioned that they are influenced by those who have specific knowledge about a subject, who are confident and competent yet aware of and willing to admit what they don't know.

We are influenced by those who share their humanity, who give part of themselves. The best professional speakers, for example, are those who are not afraid to share personal stories and reveal their vulnerability.

Personal Influencing Quotient (PIQ)

To "test" your success at influencing others, answer "yes", "no", or "I don't know" to the following questions:

- Do others perceive me the way I want to be perceived?

- Are my actions consistent with my words?

- Am I as effective in my interactions with others as I would like to be?

- Have I developed a professional network of people whom I support and who support me?

- Do I know how to give and receive feedback that improves interpersonal relationships?

- Do I practice active listening skills on a regular basis?

- Are my expectations for myself and others clearly defined and communicated?

- Do I try to better understand different points of view by putting myself "in the other person's shoes"?

- Am I willing to admit responsibility when I'm involved in a conflict situation?

- Do I create an environment that brings out the best in people?

- Do I make a difference in other people's lives?

If you did not answer a definite "yes" to each question, then this book is for you. By reading the pages that follow, you will learn new strategies for increasing your interpersonal effectiveness. At the same time, you will learn how to enhance your existing skills in influencing others.

Influencing Strategies

The ability to influence others is truly an art. Although it employs a variety of skills, influencing draws primarily on our ability to understand ourselves and others.

To communicate my strong belief in the power and importance of developing interpersonal skills, I have chosen visual art as a metaphor for influencing. Just as the artist starts with a vision when he or she sees a blank canvas or a lump of clay, so do we as individuals have a picture in our minds of who we are, who we want to be, and how we want to relate to and interact with others. To bring his or her vision to life, a painter decides the proper "mix" of colors, pulling just the right amount of color from each of the "daubs" on the palette. In a similar fashion, we as influencers must decide on the appropriate mix of strategies and behaviors to achieve our desired results.

As you read through the nine influencing strategies, you might say to yourself, "I know that. So what's new?" You may be right; however, as the character of the Stage Manager in Thornton Wilder's play *Our Town* tells the audience, "...there are some things we all know, but we don't take'm out and look at'm very often." In our busy and hectic lives, we all too often forget the basics or, at best, practice them inconsistently.

Throughout this book you will have the opportunity to examine how perception, attitudes, values, and behavior affect the communication process. You will also learn about some tips and techniques to improve your relationships with others, professionally and personally, by strengthening skills such as active listening, giving feedback, communicating expectations, developing a network, and resolving conflict, to name a few.

Each chapter details a particular strategy, including specific techniques or approaches. The strategies are arranged to form the acrostic INFLUENCE:

> Image
> Networking
> Feedback
> Listening
> Understanding
> Expectations
> Negotiation
> Communication
> Empowerment

As you read through the book, think about situations in which you would like to influence others in both your professional and personal life. Who do you want to influence? Why do you want to influence them? When could you apply these strategies?

The artist creates a masterpiece spawned by his or her burning passion for truth and beauty and an uncontrollable desire to express it. We, too, can express our passion for life and those around us by fine-tuning our interpersonal skills and mastering *The Art of Influencing.*

Strategy #1: Image

Example is not the main thing in influencing others. It is the only thing.

Albert Schweitzer

Perceptions

We hear and read a lot every day about image. Politicians, corporations, movie stars, even countries are concerned about image. Image is also important to each of us in our daily lives - both personally and professionally. Image is the *perception* others have of us. How others perceive us is determined by several factors including our appearance, the way we communicate, and what we do and say.

We must decide what image we want to project, that is, how we want to be perceived, and then develop a plan to create and maintain that image. We need to ask ourselves daily, "What is my intent?" Then ask, "How am I being perceived?" Very often, the answers to those two questions are quite different. In that case, we are lacking a very important ingredient in our ability to influence others - congruence. Congruence can be summed up in trite statements like "walk the talk" and "practice what we preach." In short, the words, actions, and appearance all match.

Congruence

Corporate America is a wealth of examples of both congruence and incongruence. The Disney organization has created an image as a friendly, clean, wholesome family-oriented organization. Every part of that organization supports and promotes that perception. If you have ever visited Disney World, Disneyland, or Epcot Center, you will notice that employees or "cast members" as they are called, are always friendly and knowledgeable, constantly cleaning the grounds, and going out of their way to help "guests" or customers. The "cast members" who portray Mickey, Goofy, Cinderella, and the dozens of other Disney characters are NEVER seen out of costume. "Cast members" enter the world of fantasy in underground rooms so that the public never sees the reality behind the illusion. Think how incongruent it would be if Disney projected an image of quality and service in their advertising, yet when "guests" visited one of the theme parks, the grounds were strewn with litter and characters were seen walking around the park only partly in costume.

I remember attending a workshop by a well-known speaker who on the stage was engaging, inspiring, warm, and friendly, yet when I approached him after his presentation to tell him how much I enjoyed the session, he was aloof and cold. He avoided eye contact, didn't smile, and gave the impression that I was imposing.

Several years ago I was president of a professional organization and was approached by a speaker who specialized in executive image. Not only did he speak about image, he wrote a book and a weekly newspaper column. His proposal and sample letter of engagement he sent to me were produced on a dot matrix printer with several typos. Needless to say, we did not use him.

Incongruence has been the downfall of many companies. Because I often speak and conduct workshops on customer service, I'm always looking for both good and bad examples from the ranks of front-line service providers. I was at the mall one day buying a few new outfits before going to a conference. I headed for one of the major department stores well-known on the East coast. Pressed for time, I quickly grabbed several items from the racks and raced into the fitting room. I was stopped in my tracks by an unfriendly attendant who yelled, "Hold it!" and pointed to the sign that read, "Only 3 Items Are Permitted in the Dressing Rooms." I knew, of course, that I was a bit over my limit, but explained that I was in a hurry and that I would bring out the same number of items I took in. She abruptly told me that it was store policy and there were no exceptions. I responded that I understood she was just doing her job but suggested that she pass on to the "powers above" that if the retailers want people to buy merchandise, then they should make it easy for people to do so. About that time, a sales associate came by. Overhearing part of the conversation, she demanded to know what my problem was. I repeated my suggestion but was cut short with "We don't make the policy. We just enforce it." At that point, I put down my items, went to the competitor at the other end of the mall, and bought the same merchandise I had intended to try on in the first place.

In contrast, a week later I once again found myself in a store in another state with a similar scenario of more items to try on than are "permitted" in the dressing room. This time the situation was different. This time the sales associate said, "Oh, that's okay. I see you have four items instead of three. And if you need another size or color, just yell and I'll be happy to get it for you." I was determined not to leave the store without buying something because the sales associate made me *want* to buy by creating a positive environment.

But what about security? In the first scenario, the store personnel were absolutely right in enforcing a policy that they were forced to put into place to help curb shoplifting. I couldn't agree more; however, it was the way in which the situation was handled that created the incongruence. I would have reacted much differently if the fitting room attendant had suggested that she hold on to the extra items and would be happy to hand them to me as I tried on and eliminated others. I would have been happy that I didn't have to get undressed and dressed several times, and the enforcement of store policy would have remained in tact.

On an individual level, think about your own reaction to people who are not what they seem. One of my biggest disappointments was when I had the opportunity to go back stage after a concert and meet a well-known singer who had been a favorite of mine for many years. As a teen, he had been a real idol, a heartthrob - so handsome and talented. When I met him my image of him was crushed. He was arrogant, overbearing, pompous, and thoroughly obnoxious.

What about parents who say, "I love you" to their children but deliver a very different message by their behavior? My husband and I were on a flight from Cozumel. A family of four was seated in front of us. One of the children, a boy about ten years old, was filling out the Customs Declaration form and printed his name in the space marked "signature." His mother yanked the form from his hands and yelled, "You're not in school! You'd better understand this is the real world. This looks like a piece of crap!" What kind of message do you think that little boy received? Furthermore, that humiliating incident may end up being the most memorable moment of his family vacation.

As mentioned earlier, others' perceptions of us often begin with our appearance. Let's look at image and personal presence from a personal point of view, starting with the basics.

Appearance

People form an impression of you within the first few seconds. That impression helps them make decisions about you, your competence, credibility, and so forth. Appearance includes your physical presence such as how you dress, your body language, and grooming. We've all heard that "you can't judge a book by its cover." But many people do. If you ever doubt this, observe how differently you are treated when you are dressed up or in jeans and a sweatshirt.

The first place to start in addressing your appearance is with what you wear. The following are simple guidelines to follow in packaging your product - you:

- Inventory your wardrobe, identifying core pieces that you can mix and match. Your goal is to build your wardrobe around certain pieces and colors.

- Buy quality. Look for quality construction and good fabric in natural fibers such as cotton, silk, wool, or blends.

- Choose accessories at the time you buy an outfit and once again, focus on quality. Choose jewelry in gold or silver or good costume pieces.

- Select a good dry cleaner.

- Know a good salesperson, someone you can rely on to help you select good pieces and will be honest in telling you if something looks good on you or not.

- Engage the services of an image consultant or check large local department stores that offer free consulting services.

I learned a valuable lesson early in my professional business career. In 1978 I switched careers from English teacher to banker. I was hired as a management trainee for a small bank in upstate New York. Seven months after starting, I was promoted to assistant branch manager at a new suburban location. About nine months later, a branch manager's position became available and based on my performance, I was fairly confident I would be promoted. Imagine my surprise and dismay when I learned that the young man, who had started as a trainee the same day as I, received the position instead. The vice president of human resources came to see me. I'm sure he knew I was upset and disappointed. I asked him what I needed to do so that I would be ready when the next manager's position became available. "Nothing," he said, "you're doing a great job. Just keep doing what you're doing." I responded by asking, "If I'm doing such a great job, then why didn't I get the promotion?" He continued to evade the issue, but I wouldn't let it rest. Finally, he said, "Well, Karen, it's the way you dress. The way you dress now is great, but when you first came to the bank, you looked like you were going to a cocktail party instead of a place of business, and that's the image senior management has of you." Of course, I was devastated but grateful that he leveled with me. The good news is that I was promoted the next year, but my poor judgment and inappropriate wardrobe selection cost me an opportunity.

One of the most important things to keep in mind about appearance is consistency. To paraphrase Susan Bixler, professional image expert and author of *The Professional Image*, if you are neat and tidy one day and a mess the next, people don't know who you really are. You're sending mixed messages.

When choosing clothing, you must not overlook the importance of color and the effect various colors have on people. Choose colors appropriate not only to you and your personality but also to the situation. Once again, I learned the hard way. I had just finished conducting a management development training session for about fifty bank branch managers and was reviewing the end-of-session evaluations after the program. One participant gave me very low scores on all aspects of my presentation. The only comment he provided was that he didn't think I should have worn a red suit. He was apparently so offended by my choice of colors that he went to the director of the program and complained to her. She explained that she had suggested that I wear a brighter color because the background in the front of the lecture hall was black, and my usual dark "banker colors" of black, navy, and gray made me fade into the background. He told her he didn't care. He had attended a program somewhere else and learned that red is an aggressive color and, therefore, found it inappropriate for a presenter or instructor to wear red in front of a group.

A challenge to business people everywhere today is the growing trend of "dress-down days." In fact, many organizations are relaxing their dress code overall, permitting employees to dress casually every day. A less restrictive dress code, however, is not a license to be sloppy or unprofessional. "Business casual" is the appropriate standard. For women, this means slacks or a skirt with a blouse or sweater, and flats rather than high heels. A man's business casual look is created by getting rid of the tie and coat, perhaps wearing a sport coat instead.

Modeling the Way

Whether you realize it or not, you are a role model for someone. If you are a parent, you're a role model for your child. If you're a manager, you're a role model for your employees. I believe that modeling the behavior you expect from others is a powerful influence. Have you ever heard someone say, "Do as I say not as I do"? What kind of message does that send? Think about your role as a parent. Do you tell your children to be honest and not cheat on tests then laugh over dinner conversation about "pulling one over on Uncle Sam" when you file your income tax return?

In my management development sessions, I ask people how they learned to manage, and the answer is that they learned from those who managed them through the years, including parents and teachers. Some were good role models; many were bad.

As William Bennett relates in *The Book of Virtues*, "There is nothing more influential, more determinant in a child's life than the moral power of quiet example." This quiet example goes well beyond our childhood years and is an integral part of every aspect of our personal and professional lives.

A role model is someone you would like to emulate. As children we selected role models that changed as we went through various developmental stages. Little girls want to be like their mommies and little boys copy daddy. As we get older, our role models become movie stars, recording artists, sports figures, or maybe a teacher. The power of role models cannot be overlooked. The advertising executives on Madison Avenue understand that power, which is evident by the number of athletes and media personalities who are paid to endorse products.

We may have no idea what lives we touch. As parents, teachers, managers, and colleagues, our success or failure as role models is determined by our value system and code of ethics which are reflected in both what we say and what we do.

Ethics

Ethics can be defined as both a set of high moral principals and behavior. Ethics are based on our value system. Values define who we are; ethics are what we do. Values help us set priorities and ethics set boundaries for behavior. Thus, ethics are value-driven, behavior-oriented, and situational. Ethics are tied to our own code of conduct. Ethical behavior involves telling the truth, keeping your word, treating others fairly, adhering to rules, and demonstrating loyalty.

On an organizational level, ethics are tied to policies and procedures that determine how employees behave. For example, organizations that value customer service will expect their employees to behave in a way that puts the customer first. On a personal level, a person who values honesty, for example, will not cheat on his or her income tax return.

Sometimes there may be an inconsistency between values and behaviors. This might be a result of not knowing what our values are, or other people or circumstances forcing us to act inconsistently.

Ethical behavior is a tricky concept and because it is values-based, that behavior will differ from person to person. A few years ago, I was teaching a graduate course on entrepreneurism at a local university. One of the sessions dealt with ethics. The majority of people in my class were people with internal corporate training responsibilities and taking the course as an elective to find out more about starting their own consulting businesses sometime in the future. I posed a number of ethical dilemmas and was quite surprised to find out that what I thought was pretty clear-cut was seen quite differently by most of the people in the class. For example, I raised the following issues:

> *Scenario #1:* A consultant subcontracts with Acme University to deliver a five-part supervisory training program for a group of twenty first-line supervisors in your organization. As the internal training consultant, you would like to repeat this program, but instead of going through Acme University, you know you could save some money by dealing with the consultant directly and having him or her deliver the program with no "middle person" involved. Is it ethical for the consultant to take the contract?

Scenario #2: You hire a consultant to deliver a two-day leadership program. You would like to offer this program to every manager in your organization but don't want to pay the consultant to deliver the program each time. Because you are a skilled trainer and attended the program yourself, you decide to take the materials, reproduce them, and deliver the program yourself. Is that ethical?

Scenario #3: You ask five different consultants to submit detailed proposals, including sample workbook pages, for a customer service program. After you have received all the proposals, you tell each consultant that you have decided to put the project on hold. Instead, you develop a program yourself, using all the consultants' materials. Is that ethical?

We had a very lively discussion, and I was quite surprised that I seemed to be the only one who found all three situations to be unethical. In the first scenario, they argued that they had now established a relationship with the consultant, and not only would the direct dealing save the company money, but the consultant would probably make more as well. In scenario #2, they believed that because they paid for the program the first time, they had a right to use the materials indefinitely. Addressing the third scenario, they felt perfectly justified in "doing research" so they could develop their own programs.

As you can see, ethical behavior is not a cut-and-dried issue. Other behaviors that may be questionable include "bad-mouthing" the competition, disclosing confidential information, misrepresenting your credentials or expertise, or using company resources (copying, telephone calls, supplies) for personal use. Although people may have different standards for their behaviors, before making a decision, think about how it might be perceived and what impact that is going to have on the image you want to project.

Etiquette

A much overlooked but important part of image is good old-fashioned etiquette. There is never an excuse for bad manners or poor conduct, from table manners to introductions.

Do you remember dictums such as "don't put your elbows on the table" or "don't talk with your mouth full"? Look around you the next time you're in a restaurant or even the company lunchroom. Table manners seem to have undergone the same fate as the dodo bird. In the so-called "good old days" people learned these basic tenets of social behavior at the dinner table. With diverse life styles, dual career families, fast food eateries, and television, many families don't even eat together.

In today's competitive environment, a polished professional employee is the most cost-effective way for a business to generate positive public relations. Image does make a difference. In fact, many MBA programs include business etiquette courses as part of the core curriculum. Many corporations hire consultants to offer programs on business etiquette to their employees. According to Letitia Baldridge, author of *Letitia Baldridge's Complete Guide to Executive Manners*, "good manners are cost-effective because they not only increase the quality of life in the workplace, contribute to optimum employee morale, and embellish the company image, but they also play a major part in generating profit." Good manners are good for business and contribute to creating a particular image. An atmosphere in which people treat each other with courtesy and respect is one in which people enjoy working and customers enjoy doing business.

Several factors influence and contribute to the growing need for good etiquette. Our growing global marketplace has resulted in fewer boundaries and more international players. More and more, we interact and do business with people from cultures quite different from our own. Even in the United States, our diverse workforce presents more challenges as more women and minorities enter the picture. The old rules and guidelines for behavior no longer apply.

As business becomes more socially oriented, companies look increasingly to those men and women who possess class and style to represent their company publicly. Unfortunately, many people, even in management positions, lack the poise, confidence, and skills necessary to succeed in business-related social situations.

There are many excellent etiquette books on the market for use in both your professional and personal lives. For business, I recommend *The Prentice-Hall Complete Guide to Business Etiquette* by Barbara Pachter and Marjorie Brody.

My purpose for including etiquette in this book is merely to heighten your awareness that etiquette plays an important role in creating your image. In fact, in today's competitive environment, hiring decisions are often influenced by a person's display of good manners and social skills. When I was a branch manager at a bank in upstate New York, I was often asked by the vice president of human resources to take management trainee candidates to lunch as a part of the selection interviewing process. I reported back to the decision-makers on the candidate's ability to handle himself or herself at a business lunch. More than one candidate didn't make the cut based on his or her performance in the dining room.

As we examine a few of the areas where you might want to polish your skills so you can be more effective in your social and business interactions, keep one important overriding principle in mind: let good manners be your guide. By that I mean never embarrass or make the other person feel uncomfortable. There are times when you will need to do the right thing instead of doing things right.

Dining Do's and Don'ts

Points of etiquette are dynamic, changing with the culture and sometimes the situation. The influx of women, technology, and people from other cultures have changed the way we look at and practice good etiquette. Although etiquette practices are constantly evolving, some things never change. In George Washington's *110 Rules of Civility and Decent Behavior*, we are told that "If You Cough, Sneeze, Sigh, or Yawn, do not Loud but Privately" and "Speak not in your Yawning, but put Your handkerchief or Hand before your face and turn aside." We might also be guided by his words dealing with who goes through a door first: "When you meet with one of Greater Quality than yourself, Stop, and retire especially if it be at a Door or any Straight place to give way for him to Pass." Finally, your mother was only following the teachings of George when he wrote, "Put not another bit into your Mouth til the former be Swallowed let not your Morsels be too big for the Gowls."

A good place to start with dining etiquette is the table setting. Regardless of age, gender, culture, or family practice, learn how to set a table correctly and then you will know what to do in any situation. As a rule of thumb, forks (salad, entree) go on the left; knives and spoons (soup spoon, teaspoon) on the right. In Western culture, choosing the appropriate utensil is easy: work from the outside in. If you should be faced with something you have never seen before (e.g. fish fork or sauce spoon), think about it and do what is logical or, if you're really uncertain and uncomfortable, watch what your dining companions do.

Use the following self-assessment to "test" your knowledge of dining etiquette:

Please answer "true" or "false" to the following questions:

1. If you are a non-drinker and your guest orders a drink, it is okay to simply tell the server you don't want anything to drink.

2. You may never dunk pieces of bread in sauces on your plate.

3. When eating soup, you move the spoon in the bowl away from you.

4. When taking your seat, you should move to the right of the chair.

5. It is never acceptable to put your elbows on the table.

6. You should thank the server every time he or she brings something.

7. When you are finished eating, it is acceptable to gently push your plate to one side.

8. During the meal, you should wipe your lips each time before your drink.

9. You should put your napkin on your lap after the food arrives.

10. Business conversation should be introduced smoothly as soon as the food order is taken.

11. Your guest should order first.

12. If you need to get up during the meal, you should put your napkin on your chair seat.

13. If you drop a utensil during the meal in a restaurant, you should pick it up and ask for another.

14. If a client orders an appetizer, it is not necessary for you to do so as well.

15. It is acceptable to eat shrimp in a shrimp cocktail without cutting it.

16. When finished eating soup, you should leave your spoon in the soup bowl.

17. It is acceptable to put used silverware on the table.

18. You should place your knife and fork together on your plate when you are finished eating.

Answers: *1-F, 2-F, 3-T, 4-T, 5-F, 6-F, 7-F, 8-T, 9-F, 10-T,*
11-T, 12-T, 13-F, 14-F, 15-T, 16-F, 17-F, 18-T.

How did you do? If you did not answer them all correctly, then you may want to consider "boning up" on your dining etiquette before your next social or business dining occasion.

Paying the Bill

Sometimes paying the bill can be tricky. In order to avoid any awkwardness or embarrassment, use the following suggestions:

- If you are the host and you want to avoid the "hassle" when it comes time to pay the check, arrange beforehand to have the bill given to you.

- When you receive the check, look it over quickly and present your credit card.

- If you are dining with associates, and each person is paying individually, the least complicated approach is to have one person pay, and the rest of the party "ante up" after you all leave the restaurant. Another alternative is to split the check equitably among all the diners with either cash or credit card. In either case, it is acceptable to ask for separate receipts. Whatever you do, don't go through the tedious and embarrassing process of calculating to the cent each person's share. I will never forget an experience I had a number of years ago. Eight of us, from different organizations in different parts of the country and all on separate business expense budgets, attended a team meeting on a weekend. After a difficult day of strategic planning, we decided to unwind at an elegant restaurant. When it came time to pay the check, our team leader grabbed the check, brought out paper and pencil and proceeded to spend the next twenty minutes calculating to the penny each person's share of the bill. She then insisted that each of us present individual credit cards to the waiter. The seven of us were quite embarrassed and did our best to "slink" out of the restaurant as quickly as possible.

Introductions

Many people are confused or at least uncertain about how to handle introductions. Perhaps you have even found yourself in a situation in which the introductions seemed awkward or did not go as smoothly as you would have liked. To master the art of introductions, follow these simple guidelines:

- Use the "senior" person's name first. For example, when introducing a younger person to an older person, say the older person's name first; junior executive to a senior executive, say the senior executive's name first; fellow executive to a customer or client, the client's name first. When introducing a man to a woman, the tradition of saying the woman's name first still prevails, unless it is a business-related situation which is then dictated by the "senior" position.

- Explain who people are when you are introducing them. For example: "Mr. Jones [a client], I'd like to introduce Jane Smith, the president of our company. Jane, Mr. Jones is the Vice President of Marketing from Acme Corporation."

- Don't use titles when introducing people of equal standing unless you are introducing an older person, a professional, or someone with official rank.

- If you forget a name, be honest about it. To cover your embarrassment or discomfort, you might say something like, "Please forgive me, but your name slips my mind at the moment. Some days I can't even remember my own."

- Offer your name quickly if you think your host forgot it. Don't be a slave to proper etiquette. The right thing to do in this case is to avoid creating an awkward or uncomfortable situation.

- Use first names only if you're absolutely sure the person prefers it. Another approach is to ask if you might use the person's first name. If you're comfortable doing so, you might say, "Mr. Jones, do you mind if I call you Richard?"

Handshakes

Handshakes can also pose a dilemma for some people. Both business and social protocol dictate the use of the handshake as the most common and preferred form of greeting. A firm handshake conveys power and confidence. Simply extend your hand at a slight angle with your thumb up. When you connect with the other person, put your thumb down and wrap your fingers around the person's palm. Give a firm handshake pumping two or three times. At the same time, you say something like, "It's a pleasure to meet you." Don't grasp fingertips or cover the other person's hand with your other hand, creating a "sandwich" effect.

Another issue that presents a stumbling block for men and women alike is who opens the door for whom and who goes first when entering or exiting an elevator, escalator, revolving door, or taxi. My purpose in this book is not to address these practices in detail. Once again, I refer you to Pachter and Brody's book for specifics. The important thing to remember is that in a business situation, gender is not a factor. In the business world, the rules of common sense and courtesy apply.

The need for proper etiquette or appropriate behavior applies also to our business environment including how we conduct ourselves on the telephone, on voice mail or e-mail and in letters and memos. Our behavior in meetings and on business trips all contribute to creating a particular image. That's why it's so important to determine what we want that image to be and then conduct ourselves accordingly. Many a career has been ruined as a result of poor judgment regarding personal conduct.

Self-image and Self-esteem

Self-image is how one sees oneself, and self-esteem is how one feels about oneself. Many factors throughout our lives, starting with early childhood, contribute to how we see and feel about ourselves, positively or negatively. Both self-image and self-esteem are created by the messages we have heard from the significant people in our lives and the experiences we have had. The way in which we internalize these messages and ascribe meaning and importance to them can have a major influence on our behavior.

Listen to the Applause

Unfortunately, many people go through life being miserable and making others miserable because of their dysfunctional behavior linked to low self-esteem.

I personally witnessed an interesting, but sad, example of low self-esteem and the profound impact on its "victim." I was conducting a week-long train-the-trainer program that included in the design an individual facilitation piece on the fourth day of the five-day session. Earlier in the week, one of the participants mentioned several times that she suffered from low self-esteem and shared unsolicited incidents from her childhood that contributed to her feeling valueless as a person. I did not realize the extent of her low self-esteem until she was asked to facilitate a twenty-minute training activity. She was the next-to-the-last person to present. When she finished, the entire group clapped just as we had done for every other participant. As with the others, I began the feedback by asking Sue what she did well and what she would like to have done better. Like many of the others, she found it difficult to say anything positive about herself but was quick to offer self-criticism. The most surprising thing was what she said next: "I'm the only one no one clapped for." Of course, that was not true, and the participants were quick to assure her that we all did indeed clap when she finished. She followed by saying that she didn't hear the clapping. Her self-esteem was so low that she was unwilling or unable to hear the applause or any of the positive feedback others were giving her. That incident underscored for me that so often we listen selectively only for the negatives. As I shared with Sue in a later private conversation, listen to the applause and the other positive feedback. The positive strokes are there if we just allow ourselves to receive them.

Before you can influence anyone else, you need to have a positive self-image and self-esteem. The following are a few tips to help you develop and maintain a positive perception of yourself:

- **Set realistic goals.** Goals need to be specific, measurable, attainable, realistic, and time-bound. You also need to establish both short-term and long-term goals. Studies show that the most successful people in the world set goals and then establish and follow a game plan to meet those goals.

- **Become self aware.** Focus on good points and be realistic about your weaknesses. Evaluate your need for and ability to change. To help you in this process, you might try completing a self-assessment instrument or ask a trusted friend or colleague to give you feedback.

- **Make time for yourself.** In our fast-paced society and demanding life styles, it's difficult to set aside time to enjoy your own company. Spending time alone to relax or indulge in a personally gratifying activity is important to both your mental and emotional health. One of the tips I share in my time management workshops is to practice

"PU" (Planned Unavailability). Just as you mark time on your calendar to attend meetings or work on a project, make an appointment with yourself devoted to self-renewal and self-reflection.

- **Learn how to be assertive,** that is, getting what you want and need without violating the rights of others. You'll learn more about how to be assertive in Strategy 8.

- **Choose to be around others who reinforce your positive self-image.** Have you ever spent time around a chronic complainer or naysayer? This person's negativity spreads like wildfire and results in bringing down everyone around him or her. Concentrate on surrounding yourself with people who will help you feel good about yourself and life in general.

- **Most important, listen to the applause!**

Strategy #2: Networking

Build good relationships and profitable transactions will follow.

Philip Kotler

Why Network?

One of the most important strategies for influencing others is networking. Networking is a supportive system of sharing information and services among individuals and groups. Recognized as the way to get things done in today's environment, networking involves various skills and activities that rely heavily on interpersonal communication. The concept and practice of networking is growing rapidly, spawned by the growing trend of corporate downsizing and organization reengineering.

Think about the successful people you know. In general, successful people are masters of networking. Networking skills help you build a base of influence by developing strong personal and professional relationships. They may be formal or informal, within or outside organizations. The benefits of networking can be summarized in three simple words: relationships, opportunities, and resources. Relationship building results in both personal and professional enrichment. The people you meet and who become part of your network are valuable sources of information about your industry, profession, other people, and even organizations. They are resources for gaining access to people and a source for referrals and business leads.

Building a Network

Networking is an organized effort and a long-term strategy that requires work. Networks need to be developed, maintained, and nurtured so that you can activate them when appropriate. Networks build and expand over time and cannot be rushed.

If networking is a fairly new concept to you or one you are not entirely comfortable with, you might start by writing down the names of people who are already in your network, although you may not realize it. Begin by creating two categories: personal and professional. Next create sub-categories. For example, under personal, you might have categories such as friends, personal services (hairdresser, tailor, shoe repair, dry cleaner), and professional services (lawyer, bankers, physicians, dentist, accountant). Include in the professional sub-category clients, peers, bosses, subordinates, competitors, and colleagues in your own and other organizations. After you have created the categories, list the names of the actual people in these roles. Are there any gaps?

Expand your network by joining professional organizations, school alumni associations, community groups, church activities, and volunteer activities. Although time-consuming, these involvements do pay off. When I moved from Rochester, New York, to the Philadelphia area, I was faced with the task of starting my business all over - this time from scratch. I knew no one and no one knew me. Even before I moved, I asked everyone in my network if they had any contacts in Philadelphia. I immediately began using my network in Rochester to help me establish a Philadelphia network. I got the names and numbers of the local chapter presidents of professional organizations I belonged to and began attending chapter meetings. I volunteered. In fact, I made a career of attending meetings, and it paid off. Within two years, I was president of the local chapters of the American Society for Training and Development and the National Speakers Association simultaneously. Because I had done considerable subcontracting work with the Rochester Institute of Technology in their training and development division, I asked my contact if she knew of comparable programs in Philadelphia. She put me in touch with someone at the University of Delaware to do similar work. My business was launched.

Connecting With Others

In both our personal and professional lives, we find ourselves thrown into situations where we need to interact with people we don't know. Whether we're attending a Chamber of Commerce "card exchange," client business lunch, company picnic, or meeting our son or daughter's future in-laws, we are faced with the uncomfortable situation of meeting new people and carrying on a conversation. Most people admit to dreading these events and many will go out of their way to avoid them. Yet these functions are opportunities to develop professional and personal contacts that last a lifetime.

Preparing for a Networking Event

Before attending any type of social or business situation, it is important to prepare.

- *Develop a positive mindset.* Prepare yourself mentally and emotionally for the experience. Instead of worrying about what you are going to say and being afraid because you won't know anyone there, tell yourself that this is an exciting opportunity, an adventure. Visualize yourself as confident and in control. Picture what you will wear and see yourself as cool, calm, and collected.

- *Do your homework.* Find out everything you can about who is going to be there: what they do, where they live, what their interests are.

- *Define your purpose.* Be clear about what you want to get from the experience. Do you want to establish contacts, gain business leads, or gather information?

- *Prepare your own introduction.* Write down and practice a 20-second introduction in which you identify who you are, what you do, and maybe an interesting tidbit designed to spark interest and encourage others to ask questions. For example: "I'm Karen Lawson. I'm a consultant specializing in management development. I influence others to make a difference."

- *Prepare 2 or 3 topic questions.* You might ask people what drew them to this organization or event. You could also inquire about how far they had to travel to get there, or how long they have been involved with the organization.

The Art of Conversation

The first place to start in developing your networking strategy is to fine-tune your conversation skills. Being known as a good conversationalist can enhance your image and create or reinforce a person's impact on others. Three key words will help you shine as a conversationalist: listen, link, and learn. To master the art of conversation, your primary goal is to actively *listen* in order to *learn* as much as you can about the other person and establish a common *link*. Here are some basics to help you shine in any situation:

- *Introduce yourself.* Be assertive. Don't be afraid to walk up to a group of people or an individual and introduce yourself. If you start with a small cluster of people, move close to the group but remain on the outer perimeter. If no one notices you and asks you to join in, listen attentively to the conversation, then at an appropriate moment make a relevant comment and then give your brief introduction. Don't be discouraged if people don't welcome you with open arms. Sometimes it takes several tries to find a "fit."

I remember a rather painful experience in such a setting when I moved to a new city. I had only been in the area for two weeks and was interested in getting involved in the local chapter of a professional organization I had belonged to for several years. With a couple phone calls, I found out when and where the group was meeting, made my reservation, and drove into the big city "all by myself" and hoped I wouldn't get lost. I picked up my name tag at the registration table, took a deep breath, and walked into a roomful of strangers who were already gathered in conversational clusters. I glanced around the room and began surveying the small groups for one that looked friendly. I took another deep breath, walked up to a group of four people engrossed in what appeared to be light conversation, and introduced myself: "Hi, I'm Karen Lawson. I'm new to the area. In fact, I've only been here for two weeks." At that point, the conversation stopped. All four people looked at me as though I had two heads. One person in the group said coldly, "How nice." All four then turned away from me and continued their conversation. Feeling very uncomfortable and embarrassed, I moved away and tried to find another group. The same thing happened. At that point, I gave up and retreated to a corner until it was time to sit down to dinner. When I left the meeting that evening I vowed I would never return, but then I decided to try again the next month - similar situation, similar results. If nothing else, I'm tenacious. I decided to give the group one more chance. This time I was lucky enough to sit next to the chapter president who went out of her way to make me feel welcome and asked me to join a committee to work on a regional conference the chapter would be hosting. I did join the committee, and that step opened up many opportunities. In fact, within two years I became chapter president! That early experience proved to be a valuable lesson for me because I am much more aware of those newcomers who walk into a room, nervous and uncomfortable. I always make it a point to look for those "lost souls," walk up to them, introduce myself, and start a conversation.

- *Start or stimulate a conversation.* Begin asking open-ended questions to get people talking. Here are some possible openings you might try:

  "What do you think about...?" "How did you happen to...?" "Tell me more about...." The important thing is to get the other person to talk about himself or herself, but be careful that you don't sound like an interrogator.

- *Listen actively.* Active listening begins with a basic interest in the other person and what he or she has to say. Maintain good eye contact, and clarify and confirm what you believe you heard. We will deal with listening in more detail in Strategy 4. Remember that the greatest compliment you can pay a person is to listen. Part of listening is not to interrupt or cut the speaker short.

- *Look for commonalities.* This is the linking part. Once you have asked open-ended questions and engaged in active listening to identify common interests, the next step is to comment and link to a similar situation or idea. The following dialogue will give you an idea of what I'm talking about:

Person #1:	"Are you originally from this area?"
Person #2:	"No, I'm originally from the Midwest."
Person #1:	"Oh, really. I'm from the Midwest, too - Ohio. Where are you from?"
Person #2:	"No kidding. I'm originally from Chicago but I went to college in Ohio."
Person #1:	"What college did you attend?"
Person #2:	"I went to Kent State."
Person #1:	"I went to Mount Union, but I had a lot of friends who went to Kent, and I used to spend a lot of weekends there. Do you remember...?"

- *Avoid "I-itis".* One of the biggest mistakes people make during conversations is that they spend the majority of the time focusing on themselves, expounding on what they do or think. Good conversationalists watch their listeners for cues when they may have begun to bore others.

- *Choose appropriate topics.* Good conversationalists are also well-read and well-informed and can talk with anyone on a variety of subjects. They know when it is appropriate to talk about particular topics and include everyone in the group by bringing up topics of general interest, not limited to any specific gender or background. Think about conversations you have been involved in. Were you or others bored or uncomfortable with discussions around sports, children, recipes, or health complaints? A good conversationalist is sensitive to others and chooses topics and words that do not offend.

Business Card Savvy

Have you ever attended a networking function where someone began passing out his or her business card like a vendor giving away grocery store coupons to every customer who walked in the door? Business cards are used to help you connect with other people - to remind them who you are, where you are, and how to reach you, not as a promotional flyer. Here are some pointers for using business cards to help create the appropriate image:

- Always carry your business cards. You never know where or when a networking opportunity may present itself.

- Make sure your business cards are not soiled, bent, or out-of-date. Keep in mind the image you are trying to create.

- Don't offer your card at the beginning of a conversation. Near the end of your discussion, ask for the other person's card, and offer yours in return.

- Make notes on the backs of business cards to remind you about the circumstances and specifics of the conversation.

- Don't scatter your card about in a large group of strangers. Remember: you're not giving away product samples.

- Don't bring your business card out during a meal. Again, timing is important. Wait until the table has been cleared to exchange cards.

Mingling Magic

- *End the conversation gracefully.* One of the keys to successful mingling is to know when and how to move on. It's perfectly fine to say simply, "It's been great talking with you" and then move to another part of the room.

- *See yourself as the host.* Think of yourself in your own home hosting a party. What would you do if you had a number of guests who didn't know each other? I would hope you would make sure people became acquainted. You can assume the same role at any gathering whether or not you're in charge. As I mentioned earlier, approach those who are standing alone, spend a few minutes chatting with them to find out who they are and something about them. Then escort them to someone else you already know or may have just met and introduce them, commenting on something they may have in common. Then gracefully excuse yourself to mingle with others.

- *Sit with people you don't know.* One of the big mistakes people make when they go to a function is to sit with their co-workers or "buddies." This is particularly tempting when you haven't seen people for a while. You have to force yourself to sit with folks you don't know, or if you are sitting with a friend or acquaintance, make sure you include others in the conversation.

- *Follow-up.* Here's another opportunity to use your business card. Include your business card in a note following up on the conversation you had. Use your business card to accompany material you are sending in response to a request or when sending an article you think someone might enjoy receiving. You might wish to personalize the card by putting a slash through your name and writing something personal with a pen on the front.

Building Relationships

Building relationships takes time and effort. It involves getting to know people personally and maintaining friendly communication on a regular basis.

One of the masters of networking and building relationships is Harvey Mackay, author of *Swim With the Sharks Without Being Eaten Alive* and *Beware the Naked Man Who Offers You His Shirt*. Mackay suggests that the most valuable tool for building and maintaining relationships is the Rolodex™. He recommends that when you meet a new person, you should make it a point to find out as much as you can about that person and then record that information on the back of the person's business card or Rolodex™ card, noting interesting points or facts about the individual as well as how and where you met. This way, when you see or talk to the person again, you can pick up where you left off. People are so pleased you remembered some seemingly insignificant personal tidbit. As Mackay says, "Little things don't mean a lot, they mean everything." The key, of course, is a good system for recording the information. My dentist does a great job of recalling that information and using it to put his patients at ease. I see him once a year, yet he always asks about my children (whom he has never met) by name and specific questions about our business. Does he have a terrific memory? Maybe. But more importantly, he records those pieces of information in my file and reviews it before he walks into the examining room. For those who are more comfortable with technology, use contact management programs such as ACT!™ to maintain information on your wide network of contacts.

Once you have established the contact, you must make a concerted effort to keep in touch and continue to build the relationship. Make it a point to socialize with people you may want to influence. Here are some tips for keeping in touch and building that relationship:

- *Socialize.* Invite your new acquaintances to your home or suggest dinner at a favorite restaurant and include spouses or significant others.

- *Mail "stuff."* Send congratulatory notes to recognize some accomplishment or event in that person's personal or professional life. Mail articles or cartoons that you believe your contact may find of interest.

- *Telephone.* Place a call every so often just to keep in touch. You don't need to have a lengthy conversation - just enough to catch up on what's been going on in each other's lives and to maintain a connection.

Collaborating and Partnering

Relationships must be cultivated and nurtured. Above all, they must be reciprocal but not in a *quid pro quo* or score card fashion. If you want to create a network of people who will support you in the future, then you must be willing to be a part of others' networks.

When someone in your contact's network calls for information or advice, give it willingly. Sometimes you may have to really "put yourself out," but your genuine interest and willingness to go out of your way to help will pay great dividends - often in ways you couldn't even imagine, sometimes months or even years later. Besides, doesn't it just feel good to do something for someone else?

Sometimes you and one of the people in your network may choose to collaborate on a project or an idea. This can be particularly valuable as we move toward a more team-oriented, collaborative corporate environment. Sharing resources and combining forces will save both time and energy, creating a truly synergetic outcome.

In the world of consulting, for example, often two or more consultants will work together on a client project, drawing on the strengths and assets of each person in order to meet the client's needs.

Networking Checklist

Check your networking savvy by asking yourself the following questions. Do I...

- Always carry business cards and practice business card etiquette?

- Take every opportunity to meet new people no matter where I am?

- Have a 20-second self introduction that I can use in any situation?

- Regularly attend meetings of professional organizations and get involved in committees and other activities?

- Send congratulatory notes, memos, articles, cartoons to people I have met as well as those I would like to meet?

- Arrange networking breakfasts and lunches with my contacts on a regular basis?

- Sit with people I don't know when attending a company or other business function?

- Encourage people to talk about themselves by asking open-ended questions?

- Listen actively by maintaining good eye contact, using positive body language, and paraphrasing as appropriate?

- At the end of a conversation, know as much (or more) about the other person(s) as he/she/they know(s) about me?

- Seek out and draw others into the conversation?

- Follow up with a note or telephone call after I meet someone new?

- Let people know I appreciate their help by sending a card or thanking them on the telephone?

- Approach a small group of strangers at a social or business function and introduce myself?

- Have a system for recording contacts and noting "special" information about them?

- Keep my word when I have promised to do a favor for someone?

- Keep up to date on my reading in both topics relevant to my business as well as general subjects?

Networking takes times and energy, but it is one of the most important and personally rewarding influencing strategies you can master.

Strategy #3: Feedback

Not everything that is faced can be changed, but nothing can be changed until it is faced.

James Baldwin

In today's communications-conscious society, the word "feedback" is thrown about frequently and indiscriminately. What is feedback? What does it have to do with influencing? When should we give feedback? What is the proper way to give it?

First of all, we need to address what feedback is not. Feedback is not criticizing, degrading or belittling. Feedback is given for the purpose of changing behavior. This is where influencing comes into the picture. We can't really change another person's behavior; we can only *influence* him or her to change.

What is Feedback?

Feedback is a process by which we describe for the other person our perception of and/or reaction to his or her action. We tend to think of feedback in terms of giving information to others about *their* behavior. That's only part of what feedback is all about. The other part is obtaining information about ourselves from others and learning to become more open. When we talk about feedback, we address the process of giving and receiving.

The process of giving and receiving feedback is best illustrated by a model called the Johari Window developed by Joseph Luft and Harry Ingham in 1969. The window is created by two axis, solicits feedback and gives feedback, thus forming four quadrants.

	Information Known to Self	Information NOT Known to Self
Information Known to Others	**1** Open	**2** Blind
Information NOT Known to Others	**3** Hidden	**4** Unknown

Quadrant 1 (Open). *Quadrant 1 is characterized by information known to self and information known to others. A simple example would be physical characteristics that each can see. On a deeper level, there is a free and open exchange of information. As this arena increases in size, the level of trust between the people involved increases. In this state, ideas, information, and feelings are shared openly. The more information is shared, the more effective and satisfying the interpersonal relationship will be.*

Quadrant 2 (Blind). *Quadrant 2 includes information not known to self but known to others. This is the result of sending out information of which you are unaware such as your mannerisms or style, that is, your personality's "bad breath." Other people's perceptions of you fall into this quadrant. We all have blind spots because we don't always know what others are thinking or feeling about us. Unless this quadrant is decreased, our interpersonal effectiveness will be greatly inhibited.*

Quadrant 3 (Hidden). *Quadrant 3 contains information known to self but not known to others. This is our protective front or facade when dealing with others. We hide things about ourselves so that people will not judge us negatively.*

Quadrant 4 (Unknown). *Quadrant 4 is characterized by information not known to self and not known to others because this information (hopes, dreams, talents, untapped potential) may not have been "allowed" to surface and develop.*

To be effective in our interpersonal relationships, we need to decrease our blind spot by soliciting feedback from others. At the same time, we also want to reduce the hidden area by self-disclosing what we think and feel. This, of course, involves risk as we reveal more of ourselves. The result is a larger "open" area created by the regular practice of giving and receiving feedback and characterized by candor, openness, and sensitivity to others.

Why Give Feedback?

As implied above, the purpose of feedback is not to tear down; it must be constructive, not destructive, intended to inform and enlighten, and delivered with genuine care and concern. Its purpose is often to prevent or resolve conflict.

Feedback is fundamental to developing and maintaining relationships. Feedback lets a person know how his or her behavior feels to another and how it affects the other person. Delivered in the form of "I messages" the receiver generally recognizes the feedback as a positive attempt to communicate one's needs, wants, and concerns. As a result, the receiver is much more likely to respond positively rather than becoming defensive, combative, or uncooperative.

When Do We Give Feedback?

- *Be timely and do it frequently.* Hold the discussion at the earliest opportunity after the behavior has occurred. Letting comments and reactions build up over time will do little to improve relationships and may result in outright conflict.

- *Do it when the receiver is ready to receive it.* Feedback is the most useful when the receiver asks for it; however, that is not always going to happen. There are certain situations where you as the manager, parent, friend, or spouse feel a need to give feedback about a behavior in order to maintain a relationship, improve job performance, or help prevent that person from making a serious mistake. Keep in mind that timing is everything.

Where Do We Give Feedback?

Feedback should be given in private. In my management development workshops, I am still amazed and disturbed by the number of people who share stories about their managers delivering negative feedback in front of their coworkers.

How To Give Feedback

Keep in mind the following guidelines for effective feedback:

- *Be descriptive rather than evaluative.* Describe the observable behavior not judgments on your part. It is important to focus on behaviors that can be observed, measured, or discussed objectively. Be careful not to put the person on the defensive by generalizing or making assumptions. Take a look at the following statements:

    - "You are not interested in..."

    - "You are irresponsible."

    - "You are selfish and inconsiderate. You think you can just walk in and help yourself to anything you want."

    What's wrong with these statements? How would you react if someone said these things to you? They are statements of personal opinion and judgment, not observable behavior. Notice how much more specific and, therefore, more effective these statements are than the original:

    - "I feel frustrated when you read the paper as I'm talking to you about my day. I really need to vent."

- "When you come in late almost every day, I am annoyed because others have to cover for you, and it impacts our productivity."

- "I am angry when you borrow my calculator without asking because I have to take time away from what I'm doing to track it down."

- *Be specific rather than general.* Describe the behavior in the context of the actual situation. Feedback should describe not only observable behavior but be stated in the context of specific incidents or situations. Useful feedback is direct, honest, and concrete.

- *Discuss only behavior the person can change.* Some people have shortcomings over which they have no control. Also, there may be circumstances or situations beyond the recipient's control. For example, if someone stutters, it is unlikely that he or she can do anything about it.

- *Consider both your needs and theirs.* This approach ensures that the receiver's ego, self-esteem, and rights remain in tact. Remember to strive for a win-win situation.

- *Communicate clearly.* Check for clarity by asking the person to state his or her understanding of the discussion. Be careful not to use the question, "Do you understand?"

Feedback Model

When offering feedback, describe the event or behavior as objectively as possible. Then describe your reaction to the event or behavior, stating clearly your own feelings and emotions. Often this is the hardest part. In our society, we tend to act out our feelings and emotions rather than state them. For example, when angry, some people yell; others slam doors. Still others "clam up," choosing not to speak to the person with whom they are angry. Some people may even cry. Yet rarely do people state calmly and simply, "I'm angry." The next step is to define and state a more acceptable alternative or course of action and give a reason or a benefit for the person to change the behavior.

Use the following model to provide effective feedback:

"When you (describe behavior), I feel (hurt, angry, annoyed, etc.) because (impact of behavior). I would prefer that you (describe desired behavior) so that (positive or negative consequences)."

For example, you could use this model to deal with the behavior of a person who doesn't call to let you know he or she will be late: "When you don't call and let me know you will be home late, I feel angry because I went to a lot of expense and effort to prepare a nice meal. I would prefer that you call me as soon as you know you will be late so that I can modify my schedule and not waste money on a ruined meal."

Another benefit to using the feedback model is that it helps you gain control. Sometimes you may have to actually write down what you are going to say and practice saying it before you present it to the other person. In so doing, you can deliver your message objectively and unemotionally, thus defusing a potentially volatile situation and opening lines of real communication.

Role of Feedback in Coaching

Feedback is an integral part of the coaching process. Whether you are a manager, parent, or team member, you are a coach.

Coaching is becoming increasingly important in both our personal and professional lives. As employees become empowered and more self-directed, the manager's role becomes more of a coach and facilitator rather than the traditional directive task-assigner. To be an effective coach, a manager needs to demonstrate certain behaviors:

Coaching Behaviors

Collaborate. The manager needs to work with the employee to identify the performance problem, set standards and performance objectives, and develop a performance improvement plan. It becomes a matter of how can WE solve the problem.

Own. The manager needs to examine his/her own behavior and accept some ownership for the problem along with the employee. The manager may ask himself or herself: "Did I make my expectations clear?" "Did I provide the proper training?"

Acknowledge. The manager needs to acknowledge successes through reinforcement and also needs to acknowledge an employee's problems, feelings, and concerns.

Communicate. The manager needs to listen, give feedback, and clarify expectations. He or she needs to practice two-way communication on a daily basis.

Help. The manager needs to advise, serving as a resource person and guide to other resources. The manager also seeks help from the employee. For example, if you need to increase sales, ask your employees to help you develop a marketing campaign.

Anyone can learn to be a coach. By applying the following step-by-step process, you will improve the performance of individual team members and get the results you want.

Step One: Problem Identification. The coach describes the current undesirable performance-related behavior that is observable, measurable, non-judgmental and can be changed. A simple example is the employee who is frequently late. In describing this unacceptable behavior to the employee, you cite specific documented dates and time periods you have observed.

Step Two: Employee Response. The employee has an opportunity to explain or question. In the tardiness case, the employee may give the standard excuses or may reveal a real problem preventing him or her from getting to work on time.

Step Three: State Expectations. The coach states clearly what he or she expects of the employee. For example, the manager restates that the employee is expected to be at his or her work station and ready to work by 9:00 am.

Step Four: Get Agreement. Through a two-way communication, the coach and employee agree on the problem and the impact it has on the organization and others. If the person is frequently late, that action places additional burden on others. It also creates resentment that affects the entire office environment.

Step Five. Improvement Plan. This step is critical. The coach and employee must collaborate to identify clearly the desired behavior. The two establish goals that are specific, realistic, attainable, simple, and time-bound as well as strategies for overcoming barriers and reaching those goals.

Step Six. Gain Commitment. In this step, the employee commits to changing behavior or improving performance by stating exactly what he/she is going to do to improve the situation. The tardy employee who has difficulty getting herself/himself ready, getting her/his small children to daycare and getting herself/himself to work on time may need to get organized the night before and/or get up earlier.

Step Seven. Set Time for Next Meeting. Before concluding the coaching session, the coach and employee agree on a time to meet to discuss progress. The next meeting should give ample time for the individual to practice the new behavior, yet not so long that he/she assumes the matter is forgotten.

Step Eight. Monitor and Follow-up. It is important to monitor the employee's progress through observation and discussions. Throughout this process, the coach gives specific feedback in the form of comments, instructions, and suggestions. For example, the manager reinforces the behavior of the former tardy employee by saying, "Joyce, I've noticed that you've been to work on time every day, and I really appreciate the extra effort to make that happen." The coach may suggest how to do something better by saying, "Next time, John, try asking the customer how he/she is going to use the account so that you can offer the appropriate choices." Another example of reinforcing positive behavior may be, "Sandy, you handled that customer well. Although you couldn't give her what she wanted, you gave her a choice and allowed her to make her own decision." Immediate praise is a powerful reinforcer. If we want the behavior repeated, we need to let the person know.

Feedback and reinforcement need to be followed with recognition and rewards. Individual recognition, teamed with incentive programs, can be very effective but should be tied to organizational goals and individual performance and valued by the employee. If, for example, the organization is committed to responding quickly to customers, then we should reward the employee's efficiency in returning phone calls or resolving complaints. That reward could be public praise, special privileges, choices in flex time, schedules, vacations, or tangibles such as gifts, money, plaques, or theater tickets. The reward should depend on the person receiving it. The employee with young children may appreciate being given more scheduling flexibility, whereas someone on a limited income would value the opportunity to work overtime.

Coaching gets results. The organization benefits from improved employee performance, increased productivity and bottomline results. The employee benefits from increased self-esteem and job satisfaction. The manager benefits by meeting goals and objectives with less stress.

Coaching takes time, practice, and patience. To guide you in the process, remember that the effective coach practices the Four R's: Respect, Reinforcement, Recognition/Reward, and Role Modeling to develop peak performers and create a winning team.

Measure Your Success

One of the ways you can measure your coaching success is to solicit feedback from your employees as to how you are doing. One easy and relatively risk-free method is to ask each employee to complete a brief "agree-disagree" questionnaire - anonymously, of course. Your questions (or statements in this case) could include, but need not be limited to, the following:

My manager...

1. frequently tells me how I'm doing.

2. gives me both positive and negative feedback.

3. tells me what he/she expects of me.

4. asks my opinion and involves me in decisions that affect me.

5. keeps me informed about changes taking place in the organization.

6. does not use threats or intimidation.

7. acknowledges my extra effort with some type of praise or recognition.

8. takes the time to explain new procedures and makes sure I understand.

9. provides the training and resources I need to do my job.

10. treats me with respect.

11. is not afraid to admit his/her mistakes or to say, "I'm sorry."

Are there any areas you would like to work to improve? Another approach would be for you to respond to the list according to how you see yourself, give the same list to your employees, then compare your self-perception with the perception of others. It could be a real eye-opener.

Regardless of the outcome, you now have valuable data that reinforce the positive approach you are already using or identify areas for improvement.

Receiving Feedback

What about when the shoe is on the other foot, that is, when we are receiving feedback? Being on the receiving end is not easy, but here are some tips to help you deal with feedback that is helpful, insightful, and constructive.

- *Develop a positive mindset.* Whether you are a manager, colleague, employee, parent, friend, or spouse, keep an open mind about the feedback process. Look at feedback as an opportunity to collect important data that will help you become the person you wish to become.

- *Ask for feedback.* Keep in mind that feedback is most useful when the receiver requests the information. Make sure that when you ask for it, you are ready to accept it, both good and bad. If you don't think you can deal with it, wait until you are more emotionally capable of handling it.

- *Don't get defensive.* Try to be open. The human reaction is to become defensive. Remember: just because a person says something, it doesn't make it true. What the person is saying is neither right nor wrong. He or she is expressing only one person's reaction or perception. Along that same line, try not to internalize it. A person's feedback has nothing to do with your personal worth as an individual.

- *Check for understanding and clarification.* Use active listening statements such as "Let me make sure I understand what you're saying" then paraphrase what you think you heard. Ask the other person to give you specific examples.

Feedback is a gift, and as with any gift, we thank the giver and then decide if we want to keep it. Does it have meaning and validity? You may want to check it out by asking others if they share the same perceptions. Depending on how important or serious the feedback, you can collect different viewpoints, compare points of similarity and difference, thus creating for yourself a more objective picture.

In Strategy #1: Image, we discussed perception and its role in creating a particular image. Feedback is an opportunity to compare your self-perception with that of others and use the information to either reinforce or modify your behavior accordingly.

Strategy #4: Listening

We have two ears and one tongue in order that we may hear more and speak less.

Diogenes

The Importance of Listening

Studies show that we spend 80% of our waking hours communicating, and according to research, at least 45% of that time is spent listening. Although listening is a primary activity, most individuals are inefficient listeners. Tests have shown that immediately after listening to a ten-minute oral presentation, the average listener has heard, understood, properly evaluated, and retained approximately half of what was said. And within 48 hours, that drops off another 50% to a final 25% level of effectiveness. In other words, we comprehend and retain only one-quarter of what was said.

Why are we such poor listeners? First of all, we have never really been taught to listen. In school, we are taught speaking, reading, and writing skills, but, in general, there are no courses devoted to listening. Secondly, most people are so busy talking or thinking about what they are going to say next that they miss out on many wonderful opportunities to learn about new things, ideas, and people. A major component of the listening process is asking questions and really listening to the answers. Dale Carnegie in his book, *How to Win Friends and Influence People*, says, "Be a good listener. Encourage others to talk about themselves." By listening you'll discover what motivates your employees to do a good job and your clients to buy your product or service. By listening, you'll discover what's really bothering your spouse or children. By listening, you'll discover a lot of very interesting people in the world around you. Listening is the catalyst that fosters mutual understanding and provides us with insight into people's needs and desires so that we can connect with them.

Listening Versus Hearing

Listening is the process of taking in information from the sender or speaker without judging, clarifying what we think we heard, and responding to the speaker in a way that invites the communication to continue.

Listening is one of the most important, most underused, and least understood influencing skill. You might be wondering, "How can I influence someone through listening?" Think about it. How do you feel when someone really listens to you? My guess is that you feel respected and appreciated. When people sense that others are listening to them and trying to understand their viewpoints, they begin to open up and drop their own barriers. The result is a climate of trust, openness, and mutual respect that leads to greater cooperation.

People confuse hearing with listening. Hearing is the physical part of listening, that is, when your ears sense sound waves. Listening, however, involves interpreting, evaluating, and reacting.

Take a moment and complete the following self-test to determine your perception of your listening competence and efficiency. Ask yourself the following questions:

Do I...

- Maintain eye contact with the speaker?

- Ignore distractions while listening?

- Wait until the speaker is finished before I speak?

- Listen for tone as well as words?

- Try not to over-react to emotionally charged words?

- Listen to understand rather than spend time preparing my next remark?

- Avoid assuming what the other person means by asking questions to ensure understanding?

- Capture the main ideas rather than just the facts when taking notes?

- Refrain from "tuning out" someone I don't like or whose message is boring or contrary to my belief?

How did you do? If you really want to find out if you are an active listener, compare your perception of your listening skills with others' perceptions of you. Ask people close to you such as family members and co-workers to complete (anonymously, of course) the same assessment by responding to each item with you in mind. You might be surprised by the outcome.

Consequences of Poor Listening

Poor listening is often the cause of misunderstandings and their resulting conflicts. Many errors on the job can be traced to poor listening skills. I know of one instance where a major conflict resulted when a stock trader told the analyst to take a million dollars out of reserves and the analyst "heard" the trader say take reserves down to a million. Not only did this miscommunication destroy the working relationship between the trader and the analyst, it also created a major problem for the client.

Barriers to Listening

External Barriers

- *Physical environment.* External distractions can be almost anything that involves an outside stimulus. Noise, interruptions, and surroundings can interfere with your ability to listen.

- *Inarticulateness.* A person who is unable to express himself or herself clearly and distinctly creates a tremendous barrier for those listening. If the speaker does not speak distinctly, uses words inappropriately, or lacks clarity of thought in expressing ideas, the listener will "tune out."

Internal Barriers

- *Close-mindedness.* Have you ever tried to talk to some-one whose mind was already made up? Or how about the person who believes that he or she knows the answer? I am reminded of the person who called me one day to ask my advice on a business problem. As I started to respond to his question and share my thoughts and opinions, he cut me off by saying, "Yeah, yeah, I know...." It was clear that he already knew the answer and certainly was not willing to listen to the advice he had solicited.

- *Preoccupation.* Sometimes we just don't pay attention. We may be thinking about something else we need to do or reflecting on something that happened. In either case, the problem is that we are focused on something other than the person and the message at hand.

- *Emotional blocks.* We all have emotional reactions trig-gered by words, topics, or visual stimuli. These triggers can be positive, negative, or neutral. We tend to think that only negative responses interfere with our listening; however, all three can cause us to become poor listeners. A negative response, for example, may be elicited when the listener hears a word that makes him or her "see red." Many women, particularly in the business world, bristle at the use of the word "girl" when referring to any female over eighteen. Their emotional response is so intense that they "tune out" anything of value that the speaker may be sharing. We may also become argumentative, creating a major communication breakdown. Neutral responses can also be harmful because they result in apathy or disinterest. Surprisingly, positive emotional responses can interfere with our listening ability as well. Because we like the speaker or are enamored with his or her topic or viewpoint, we may accept at face value everything he or she is saying. Both negative and positive emotional triggers are quite evident during political campaigns. In any case, emotional triggers cause us immediately to evaluate rather than first comprehending, then interpreting, and finally evaluating appropriately.

- *Stereotyping and prejudice.* This barrier refers not only to the common prejudices we know such as race, religion, gender, etc., but prejudices we have about any specific individual. Each of us has personal listening biases regarding appearances, manners, and speech.

- *Mind-wandering.* The average person speaks at a rate of 125 words per minute. Yet an individual can think at a rate of 400 to 500 words per minute. As a result, the listener has a lot of "leisure" time during which his or her mind wanders, thinking about a variety of unrelated topics. Good listeners will use this extra time to review, reflect, and summarize the message just heard.

- *Defensiveness.* As human beings, we have very definite thoughts, opinions, and ideas. When we feel these are being questioned or attacked, we become defensive and block what the other person is trying to say.

- *Judging.* Some people have already made up their minds that the subject is either uninteresting or too difficult. As a result, they tune out.

- *Preparing your rebuttal.* Sometimes we are so anxious to "have our say" or express our opinions that we don't listen to the other person's complete message. We're too busy rehearsing in our mind what we are going to say next and trying to find the next opportunity to interject.

Active Listening Benefits

- *Keeps communication channels open.* When an atmosphere of trust and openness has been created through active listening, people are more likely to express themselves in a spirit and practice of authentic and ongoing communication.

- *Reduces friction and prevents conflicts.* As mentioned earlier, poor listening leads to conflict. We act on what we think we heard, not necessarily on what we did hear. Using active listening skills to clarify and confirm will prevent misunderstandings.

- *Provides opportunities for learning.* When we're talking, we're not learning. Active listening allows us to gather data and information we may not otherwise be exposed to. It's surprising what we can learn just by listening.

- *Generates ideas.* When people truly listen to one another, people become excited and energized. An environment that encourages people to listen and be listened to is one that ignites both the spirit and the mind and promotes creative thinking.

- *Enlists support of others.* People want and need to feel valued, that what they think and say matters. You are much more likely to support the person who supported you by really listening to what you had to say.

- *Builds and strengthens personal and professional relationships.* Because both people are open and receptive to producing clear communication, they are able to work together more effectively.

- *Prevents misunderstandings.* As mentioned earlier, we act on what we think we heard, not necessarily what the person meant. If we practice active listening techniques, we ensure that the message sent and received is the same.

- *Prevents or reduces errors in work.* For the same reasons as discussed earlier in the prevention of misunderstandings, active listening will prevent errors. Active listening, therefore, has a positive impact on the bottom line.

- *Sells ideas or products.* Listening can improve sales. By actively listening to our customers and clients, we can determine what they really want and need. Listening makes it easier to tie benefits to the customer's needs.

- *Makes better decisions.* Active listening enables us to absorb and evaluate all the information presented, not just what we may want to hear. When we have all the facts and details, we are in a much better position to make a rational, informed decision.

Poor Listening Habits

In addition to the barriers mentioned above, many people have developed poor listening habits over the years.

- *Interrupting the speaker.* There are many reasons people interrupt, including impatience, but most of all, lack of self-discipline.

- *Not paying attention.* Sometimes we give the appearance of listening but the mind is focused on a totally different topic or conversation.

- *Feeling defensive.* People who are defensive assume they know the speaker's intent and are ready to launch a counter attack.

Active Listening Guidelines

Because our listening speed is faster than the other person's speaking speed, there is a lot of "dead" time in the communication process. Often, we fill that void by daydreaming or doing something else like making a "to do" list or doodling. Instead, try using the time to process what the speaker has just said in order to reach a deeper level of understanding.

- *Be aware of your own biases.* It's important that we recognize our own biases regarding subject matter or even our responses to people's backgrounds or appearance. Simply put, keep an open mind.

- *Identify your emotional triggers.* Certain words or complete messages, ideas, or philosophies can easily arouse our emotions. If you doubt this, just think about your emotional response the next time you hear a politician whose ideology is the opposite of yours.

- *Be empathetic and nonjudgmental.* Each of us is different with our own quirks and peculiarities. Instead of focusing on distracting behaviors, concentrate on what the speaker is saying. At the end of one of my training sessions with a group of bank branch managers, one of the participants gave me a very negative evaluation because he didn't like my eye make-up. Remember my red suit incident? In both cases, the participants were not able to concentrate on what I had to say because they were too absorbed with what was for them a distraction caused by something in my appearance.

- *Learn to separate fact from opinion.* Avoid jumping to conclusions or making assumptions - warranted or not - about what the other person means. Check it out first.

- *Listen for the feeling of what is being conveyed.* Be aware of nonverbal cues such as gestures, facial expressions, and posture.

- *Take notes.* According to a Chinese proverb, "The palest ink is better than the best memory." No matter how good your memory, you cannot possibly remember everything. Don't, however, attempt to write down every word. In doing so, you are focused on the notetaking process rather than the listening process.

- *Listen for the main idea or thought.* Try to capture in your mind and then put on paper the essence of what the speaker is saying.

- *Give your full attention.* Look the speaker in the eye, lean forward, and encourage the speaker to continue by nodding your head and making verbal comments such as "That's interesting," or "Tell me more." Even if you find the speaker or the message boring, try to find an area of interest in the speaker's message.

- *Don't interrupt.* This is a tough one if you have developed that habit. Try to concentrate and inhibit your tendency to interrupt.

- *Limit your own talking.* You can't talk and listen at the same time. The ancient Greek philosopher Diogenes put it well when he said, "We have two ears and only one tongue in order that we may hear more and speak less."

- *Pay attention to nonverbal cues.* Observe body language. Be patient and sensitive to the other person's feelings and reactions. A number of years ago when I was a bank manager, a vendor dropped into my office and asked if he could talk to me for a few minutes. He spent the next 45 minutes talking at me, telling me all the wonderful things his company could do for me. He never once acknowledged the fact that my body was tensing, my jaw was set, and I was definitely frowning. He was so intent on delivering his message that he ignored the nonverbal cues that I had "tuned him out."

Active Listening Techniques

Active listening is a two-way process and a shared responsibility. In many of my management, customer service, and communications workshops, I use a simple but effective activity called the "Paper-tearing Exercise" to illustrate this point. First I distribute a sheet of paper to each participant, then I give the following instructions:

- "Please pick up your sheet of paper and close your eyes."

- "Listen carefully and follow my instructions."

- "Please keep your eyes closed during the entire activity."

- "Fold your paper in half. Tear off the upper right-hand corner."

- "Fold your paper in half again. Tear off the lower left-hand corner."

- "Fold your paper in half once more. Tear off the lower right-hand corner."

- "You may now open your eyes and open your papers."

Participants hold up their papers, and we all have a good laugh because each person's sheet of paper looks different. I then ask what went wrong. Most people immediately say that it was my fault because I didn't give clear instructions. Generally, someone sees the light and suggests that they could have asked questions to clarify how I wanted the paper folded, that is, if the fold was to be on the top, bottom, or one of the sides, and if the paper was to be folded horizontally or vertically. In discussing the activity further, the issue of assumptions comes up. I, as the speaker, made certain assumptions about people folding their papers the same way I do; the listeners assumed they knew what I meant or else they were too embarrassed to ask what appeared to be a "silly" question.

Clarifying and confirming

When we listen, we interpret the speaker's message and then respond according to what we think he or she said. More often than not, our assumptions are incorrect and our responses can create misunderstandings and even conflict. It is important, therefore, to clarify what we think the speaker has just said by using some of the following approaches:

> "As I understand it, what you're saying is..."
> "What I hear you saying is..."
> "I get the impression that..."

By paraphrasing the content of the message, the speaker can either confirm or further clarify the message, thus ensuring the accuracy of the communication.

Discuss implications

Sometimes you may be clear on what the speaker said but are unsure as to what he or she means. Often this is a result of an incomplete message. To further clarify intent, try to expand the discussion by using phrases similar to the following:

> "If you did that, then you would be able to...."
> "Would that mean that...?"

Reflecting underlying feelings

Listen between the lines for attitudes, feelings, and motives behind the speaker's words. Be alert to facial expressions, movements, gestures, and tone of voice. Once again, confirm your perception by saying some of the following:

> "If that happened to me, I would be upset...."
> "I can imagine that you must feel...."
> "You sound upset about the situation...."

Inviting further contribution

One very effective way of getting people to open up and share more about themselves is to ask open-ended questions - those that require more than a "yes" or "no" answer. Open-ended questions start with the words, "who," "what," "where," "when," "why," and "how." Questions starting with "why" should be used with caution because they risk coming across as challenging and may cause the other person to become defensive. "Tell me more about...." is also a powerful way to encourage people to expand their comments. Open-ended questions will help you gain valuable insight into the other person's thinking. By asking questions such as "What thoughts have you given to...?" and "How does that fit into...?", you will improve the communication interaction and enhance your effectiveness as an influencer.

Listening is hard work, but well worth the effort. Active listening will result in more effective communication and more rewarding relationships.

Strategy #5:
Understanding

A man to be greatly good, must imagine intensely and comprehensively; he must put himself in the place of another and of many others; the pains and pleasures of his species must become his own.

Percy Bysche Shelley

Understanding helps build relationships. By getting to know people personally and staying in contact with them, we develop a bond that may last a lifetime. Our ability to understand the needs and concerns of others helps us to be more effective in our daily interpersonal interactions. Through understanding we connect with others.

Values

Values are the underpinnings and basis for understanding ourselves and others. Values are the degree of importance one places on something. As we discussed in Strategy #1, values provide the basis for our ethical behavior.

Clarifying Your Values

In order to understand others, we need to understand ourselves first. A good starting place is clarifying our own values.

Let's start by taking a look at where our values come from. Our values are shaped by our environment and the people around us - first our parents, then our teachers and school environment, our friends, religious affiliation, the media, culture and geographic region in which we live, historical events taking place around us, and our own individual significant emotional events.

The time in which we live has a profound impact. Dr. Morris Massey, well-known for his work in the area of value programming, asserts that we are products of our environment. In his 1976 videotape presentation *What You Are Is Where You Were Then,* Dr. Massey tells us that our values, formed by our surroundings, are established by age ten and locked in by age twenty. Our values can be altered, however, by what Dr. Massey calls a significant emotional event.

A significant emotional event is an event or experience, positive or negative, immediate or cumulative, that has a profound impact on the individual. The death of a loved one, a divorce, or losing one's job are examples of immediate significant emotional events. Parenting is an example of a significant emotional event that is cumulative. In any case, such events result in providing us with powerful insight that ultimately leads to a change or shift in our values.

Although our values help define who we are and influence what we do, many of us have never had the opportunity to think about and examine closely what we value and why. To gain additional personal insight, use the following self-assessment to explore what's really important to you.

Values Clarification

INSTRUCTIONS: For each of the following values, indicate their degree of importance to you personally using the following scale:

> 1=*Extremely important;* 2=*Quite important;* 3=*Moderately important;* 4=*Unimportant.* Then look at those you have chosen as extremely important and put a star or asterisk by your top three choices.

_____ **Knowledge and Wisdom.**
To learn new things and ideas; personal growth through experience.

_____ **Morality and Ethics.**
To maintain a sense of right and wrong; to adhere to socially accepted standards.

_____ **Freedom and Independence.**
To be able to make one's own decisions and use one's own judgment.

_____ **Love and Affection.**
To experience a sense of caring for people and being cared for by others.

_____ **Money and Security.**
To have enough income and resources to provide for wants and needs; to feel safe in your environment.

_____ **Mental and Physical Health.**
To be free of stress, anxiety, and physical illness; to be fit and energetic.

_____ **Religious and Spiritual Beliefs.**
To believe in a supreme being or spiritual force.

____ **Friendship.**
To have a sense of belonging to a person or group; companionship.

____ **Pleasure.**
To participate in things you like to do; to have fun and enjoy life.

____ **Achievement and Accomplishment.**
To have feelings of self-satisfaction as a result of completing a task, overcoming an obstacle, or meeting a challenge.

____ **Loyalty and Trust.**
To experience a feeling of dedication and commitment to friends, family, country, organization, etc.; to have confidence in the integrity and honesty of others.

____ **Power and Influence.**
To have a sense of control and influence over yourself and others.

____ **Justice.**
To believe in a system that rewards positive behavior and punishes negative; sense of fairness.

____ **Recognition.**
To receive praise and rewards for accomplishments and contributions.

After you have reviewed your values, think about how they influence you and your behavior and interactions with others. How do others' values impact you? Your values impact decisions and choices you make every day of your life from what you wear to who you vote for. By focusing on your own set of values, you can better understand yourself and others - particularly why and how you and others make certain decisions.

Dealing With Conflicting Values

Learning how to relate to those whose values may be different from ours is both challenging and rewarding. For some, it is also disturbing. There is a tendency for us to impose our values on others. After all, our values are the right values. Right? It is particularly disturbing for some to discover that those closest to them - children, spouses, friends - may have a different set of values.

Many problems of communication, productivity, interpersonal relations, and resulting conflicts lie primarily in significantly different value systems. These conflicts can be minimized greatly if we understand and learn to accept values that are different from ours.

As Dr. Massey relates, "You have to deal with other people where the other people are, not where you would like them to be."

Developing Empathy

In its purist context, empathy is a psychological term meaning the projection of one's own personality into the mind or personality of another in order to understand him or her better. In a more pragmatic form, empathy is the ability to identify with the feelings, thoughts, or attitudes of others. Empathy is what helps me connect with every person in my classroom or audience, and empathy will help you relate to and understand your family, friends, co-workers, and others with whom you interact. Empathy not only helps us to understand but also helps us put things in perspective. Several years ago, my wallet was stolen while I was having lunch with a client. I was very upset and acted as if I had been the only person ever victimized by a thief. I felt sorry for myself until a week later when I read about all the people who lost everything they owned in a hurricane. My loss was trivial in comparison. Yet I recalled my experience and how helpless I felt, and I was able to relate to the disaster victims.

The ability to look beyond ourselves into the heart and soul of others and to identify the common bond of humanity is what empathy is all about. To paraphrase an old adage, "You can't judge a person until you've walked a mile in his or her shoes." Empathy helps us to identify with the things and people around us, to recognize ourselves in others, and others in us. Empathy cannot be taught, but it can be developed. You can develop skills and behaviors that show another person you care. Empathy skills are critical to your success as a coach-manager, teacher, parent, friend, and so forth because empathy is the foundation of the helping process.

The first step is to look inside yourself for that common emotional bond each time you communicate or interact with others - whether it be with one person or with one thousand and one. No matter what the experience, try to relate it to something that has happened to you of a similar nature. The examples and experiences are all around you in everything you do. For example, a visit to my dentist provided me with an excellent example of empathy. If you have ever had a full set of mouth x-rays, you know that it is not a fun experience. Recently, I went to the dentist for my routine cleaning and before I was poked, pierced, and sand-blasted, I had what seemed to be eighteen 2 by 4's put in my mouth. As I suffered in silence, the "torture queen" (thinly disguised as a friendly dental assistant) complimented me on my pain endurance. She mentioned that she had recently had a physician in the chair who complained every time she, the assistant, put another plate in his mouth. "You're hurting me! You're not doing it right! Ouch!" Halfway through the ordeal, the assistant stopped, looked him in the eye and said, "Just remember this the next time you put a tongue depressor down a child's throat and tell him it doesn't hurt."

The importance of empathy became quite clear to me when I asked my students at the end of a Quality Management course I was teaching, "What did you like best about this course?" Surprisingly, hands shot quickly into the air, and Carla shouted, "We loved your stories. They made the ideas and the points come alive. We could really relate to your experiences."

Of course, I loved the positive feedback, but I needed to know more, so I asked, "Why did you like my stories?" Rose answered, "Because you made it more human, and we really connected with you." That response started me thinking about my growth and evolution as a trainer, teacher, and speaker. I asked myself, "What is different about my interactions with my audiences?" Stories. I tell stories all the time to illustrate a point, to connect with my audience. I've been more effective and successful as a speaker and trainer but I never realized that it's the stories that make the difference. My stories help me connect.

As Harvey Mackay, author of *Swim With the Sharks Without Being Eaten Alive* and *Beware The Naked Man Who Offers You His Shirt*, puts it, "People don't care how much you know about them - only that you care about them." Think about your behavior - what you say and do - when you interact with others. Be aware of both your verbal and nonverbal behavior. Does your behavior convey empathy? Do you convey patience, warmth, and concern without words? To "test" your empathetic behavior, ask yourself the following questions?

Do I...

- Reach out and touch someone on the hand or arm in a soothing manner when appropriate?

- Sit down and listen attentively to what the other person is saying?

- Give messages of encouragement, support, or understanding such as "I understand that you are very angry (sad, disappointed, hurt, etc.) right now..."?

- Reflect on the other person's feelings with statements such as "You seem to be upset..." or "If that happened to me, I would be upset, too..." or "I can imagine that you must have been hurt by..."?

- Respect the other person and refrain from making statements such as: "You shouldn't feel that way" or "It will be okay"?

- Allow the other person to do most of the talking?

- Avoid telling the other person what to do with statements such as "If I were you..." or "I would..."?

Whatever you do in expressing empathy, do not say, "I know how you feel." You can imagine what the other person might be feeling, but you cannot know what he or she feels because you are not that person. Besides, that type of statement shifts the focus from the other person to you.

Keep in mind, however, that empathy is not the same as sympathy. Empathy is the understanding of emotions, whereas sympathy is the sharing of similar emotions. Sympathy carries the inherent danger of becoming too involved in another's world and emotions, making it difficult to separate yourself from the person you are trying to help and understand.

Dealing With Style Differences

An often overlooked source of misunderstanding is personality, behavior, and communication styles. There are many assessment instruments on the market including the Myers-Briggs Type Indicator (MBTI), published by Consulting Psychologists Press, Life Orientations Survey (LIFO) by Stuart Atkins, Personal Style Survey (DISC) by Carlson Learning, and "I Speak Your Language" by Drake Beam

Morin, to name a few. The purpose of these instruments is to provide you with insight into your style, as well as others, in order to improve interpersonal effectiveness. Most are based on personality theory put forth by Carl Jung in the early 1900s. Jung identified "psychological types" based on patterns of behavior. According to Jung, people follow certain behavior patterns in the way they prefer to perceive and make judgments.

Over the years, theorists and practitioners have modified, expanded, and applied Jung's theory to the development of their own instruments. If you have not done so, I highly recommend that you seek out an opportunity to complete a self-assessment instrument such as those listed above. It is a useful tool to expand self-awareness and guide you in your personal growth. It will help you to better understand yourself and others and provide insights that will be useful in resolving conflicts, strengthening relationships, and improving communication with co-workers, family, and friends.

To get a flavor for these style differences, read each of the following statements and check the ending that is most like you.

1. When I am in a learning situation, I like to...
   a. be involved in doing something.
   b. work with people in groups.
   c. read about the information.
   d. watch and listen to what is going on.

2. When I am working in a group, I like to...
   a. direct the discussion and activity.
   b. find out what other people think and feel.
   c. remain somewhat detached from the rest of the group.
   d. go along with the majority.

3. When faced with a conflict situation, I prefer to...
    a. confront the situation head on and try to win.
    b. work with the other person to arrive at an amicable resolution.
    c. present my position by using logic and reason.
    d. not to make waves.

4. In a conversation, I tend to...
    a. come straight to the point.
    b. draw others into the conversation.
    c. listen to what others have to say, then offer an objective opinion.
    d. agree with what others say.

5. When making a decision, I tend to...
    a. make a decision quickly and then move on.
    b. consider how the outcome will affect others.
    c. take time to gather facts and data.
    d. consider all possible outcomes and proceed with caution.

6. I am seen by others as someone who...
    a. gets results.
    b. is fun to be with.
    c. is logical and rational.
    d. is a calming influence.

7. In a work environment, I prefer...
    a. to work alone.
    b. to work with others.
    c. structure and organization.
    d. a peaceful atmosphere.

Now count the number of items checked for each letter. The letter with the most checks indicates your preferred style: a=Candid; b=Persuasive; c=Logical; d=Reflective. As you read the following brief descriptions, determine for yourself the accuracy of the description as it reflects your personal style.

Candid

Candid individuals are direct and controlling. They like to be in charge and the center of attention. They are action-oriented and may be perceived as pushy and domineering. They enjoy being challenged, and they tend to make decisions quickly, sometimes with little information. Those with a candid style are demanding of themselves and others.

To be more effective, the candid person needs to be more sensitive to others, practice active listening, and exercise more caution in making decisions.

Persuasive

Those whose primary style is persuasive love people. They are outgoing, warm, and animated. They are very sociable and may be perceived as overly emotional. They have a short attention span and dislike details. Persuasive individuals are spontaneous, entertaining, and like to take risks.

To be more effective, the persuasive person needs to improve organization skills and spend more time looking at the facts.

Logical

Logical individuals pride themselves on their use of analysis and reason in all situations. They have a strong need to be right, and they rely on facts and data to support their position. Although they are good problem-solvers, they are slow to make decisions. They are sometimes perceived as aloof and critical. They often ask probing questions and frequently take the opposite point of view in a discussion.

To be more effective, the logical person needs to be more flexible, spend less time gathering data, show more concern for people, and be more expressive of his or her feelings.

Reflective

Reflective individuals are reliable and cautious. They tend to be perfectionists and seek security. They avoid conflict and may be perceived by others as weak. Reflective people are good listeners and make great friends. They are loyal, cooperative, and supportive. For this reason, they are good team players.

To be more effective, the reflective person should learn to be more assertive, less sensitive, and more willing to take risks.

By understanding style differences and learning to accept and adjust to those differences, we can be more effective in our relationships with others. Not only can we influence others through our ability to adjust our style to theirs, our acceptance of them and our willingness to adapt influences others to accept and adapt to us as well.

Strategy #6: Expectations

...if we treat people as though they are what they should be,
we help them become what they are capable of becoming.

Johann Wolfgang von Goethe

Results Through Expectation

People, managers in particular, often expect - and frequently get - the worst from the people they manage. Do any of these statements sound familiar?

- Employees just don't care.

- Today's worker isn't motivated.

- They have no work ethic.

- You can't depend on people.

- If you want it done right, you have to do it yourself.

- They're lazy.

When thoughts like these run through our minds, and even worse, escape our lips, we need to look first at our own attitudes and assumptions.

Expecting The Best

> *"...The difference between a lady and a flower girl is not how she behaves, but how she's treated. I shall always be a flower girl to Professor Higgins because he always treats me as a flower girl and always will, but I know I can be a lady to you, because you always treat me as a lady and always will."*
>
> Eliza Doolittle in
> George Bernard Shaw's *Pygmalion*

The power of expectation alone can influence the behavior of others. To put it another way, a person's expectations about a future event can affect the likelihood that it will happen. This phenomenon called the self-fulfilling prophecy or Pygmalion Effect theorizes that people sometimes become what others expect them to become - good or bad. According to Greek mythology, Pygmalion created Galatea out of envy and desire and fell in love with his own sculpture of the perfect woman. In the Broadway musical and movie *My Fair Lady* (adapted from George Bernard Shaw's play *Pygmalion*), Professor Henry Higgins transforms Eliza Doolittle, a common flower girl, into an elegant lady. A very real and tragic example of the self-fulfilling prophecy is the 1932 Stock Market crash which began as a rumor of insolvency leading to a run on the banks.

The self-fulfilling prophecy may be communicated directly or indirectly. Sometimes the indirect can be far more damaging. I am reminded of an incident from my junior high school days. The school I attended grouped students by ability. As a seventh grader, I was in 7-1, the so-called "smart" group. I remember a party at my house where my mother suggested to one of my friends who happened to be in 7-8, the "dumb" group (as the other kids labeled it) that she should study harder so she could "move up." My friend, Darlene, quietly replied, "Why should I? They think I'm dumb anyway."

Although that incident happened a long time ago, I've never forgotten it. I tell that story frequently to participants in my motivation and leadership sessions to illustrate the importance of a manager's (also parent or teacher) role in influencing and shaping the behavior of others. Darlene was an example of someone "living down" to the expectations others had of her. How often do we inadvertently send similar messages to our employees when we say, "Give it a shot" accompanied by a tone of voice that says, "I don't expect much from you"? Or how about when we say to our son or daughter, "Try to do your best" in a tone that communicates "your best really isn't very good"? The self-fulfilling prophecy can be either a useful or a destructive tool in the workplace, home, or classroom. Like Shaw's Professor Higgins, the significant influencer *can* transform "losers" into "winners." When we communicate to others our high expectations of them, their self-confidence will grow, their capabilities will develop, and their accomplishments will be many. The responsibility is enormous; the challenge, exciting; and the possibilities, endless.

Communicating Expectations

In a classic experimental study conducted in the mid-1960s, researchers Robert Rosenthal and Lenore Jacobson tested the Pygmalion Effect in an elementary school in a lower socio-economic class neighborhood. At the beginning of their study, they gave the children a nonverbal intelligence test. The test was just a ruse. The researchers then chose at random 20% of the children in each class and told their teachers that these children were intellectually gifted and that their performance would most likely improve dramatically over the course of the school year. When the children were retested near the end of the year, the so-called "bloomers" showed a gain of four points over that of the other children. Rosenthal and Jacobsen found that teachers did not spend any more time with the "gifted" students, but the way in which they interacted with them, that is, the way they were treated made the difference.

Studies conducted in business and industry have had similar results, showing that a manager's high expectations lead to high productivity and low expectations result in low productivity.

Many relationships end up in serious trouble because people have not communicated expectations. Marriages, for example, often fail because the two people involved have not discussed what they expect of each other and the relationship. Even if the discussion has taken place, we need to update expectations particularly after any change such as the birth of a child, a job change, purchase of a house, or even acquiring a pet. Often we have certain expectations of our spouse or significant other but keep them locked tightly in our mind. Similarly, managers fail to communicate to their employees standards of performance and other job-related behaviors. We expect the other person to be a mind reader and when that person does not meet our expectations, we get hurt or angry.

People, both children and adults, want to do a good job. Children start school eager and enthusiastic, yet within a relatively short period of time, much of that exuberance fades. Employees bring the same positive attitude and motivation to the workplace. Have you ever heard anyone say, "I'm going to work today and do a 'bad' job"? Whether a manager, teacher, or parent, what a person expects of others and the way he or she treats them will determine the success or failure of those people in varying degrees. In their landmark book, *In Search of Excellence*, authors Peters and Waterman put it very succinctly: "Label a man a loser and he'll start acting like one." Remember my friend, Darlene?

Positive Pygmalions are those who create high performance expectations and communicate them. Studies show that when a supportive, nurturing culture is created, people do what they believe is expected of them. So how do we create such an environment?

Know What You Want

First of all, you must also know what kind of behavior you want the person to demonstrate. In other words, what do you want the person to do differently? For example: Do you want an employee to come to work on time? Greet the customers in a friendly manner? Complete forms correctly? Do you want your child to clean her room? Come straight home after school? Do you want your spouse to show you more attention? Take responsibility for planning the family vacation? You must first be clear about your expectations before you can communicate them to someone else.

There is no quick fix. Changing another's behavior takes time and patience. You will find that what works well for one person may not work for another. You may have to use "trial and error" until you identify and match the right methods to the appropriate people.

You also may have to face the unpleasant truth that no matter what you do, you might have some employees, for example, who refuse to change their behavior. If that is the case, you will have to "bite the bullet" and ask them to leave. It's very demotivating to other employees to keep someone on who will not cooperate and perform according to agreed upon expectations.

We live in a world of contracts: what I want from you and what you expect from me, both at home and on the job. People today expect to be part of the process and are no longer satisfied with receiving information on a need-to-know basis. In the work world, people want to know what the organization's plan is, how they fit into that plan, and how they're doing along the way. In a family, children want to know about decisions that are going to affect their lives. For example, if the family needs to relocate as the result of dad's or mom's promotion, the children need to be an active part of making decisions about the move and the new location.

Tell Others What You Want

In communicating your expectations to others, follow the principles and techniques discussed in the other eight strategies of this book.

As I discussed in Strategy #3: Feedback, exceptional managers communicate and measure performance in precise, objective terms. They specify speed (rate), quantity (number or amount), accuracy (absence of errors), thoroughness (completeness), and timeliness (meets deadlines). Furthermore, they focus on the positive performance they want rather than the negative consequences.

Ideally, setting and communicating expectations with an employee should be handled the very first day a new employee comes on board. However, keep in mind that it's never too late to start. When my husband, Bob, was promoted to a director in the corporation where he had worked for over twenty years, he "inherited" his secretary, also a twenty-year veteran with plenty of secretarial experience. My husband often complained that Janice was frequently away from her desk, and as a result, the phone would ring and ring. (This was in the days before voice mail). As we discovered, Bob was not alone. We were at dinner one evening with several of Bob's counterparts and their spouses. As often happens, the conversation turned to work, and all five of the managers complained about their secretaries not answering the telephone. After listening to their tirade about employee incompetence, I asked them if they had told their secretaries they expected the telephone to be picked up in three rings or have someone cover for them if they needed to be away from their desks. They responded by telling me that they didn't think they had to. After all, these were experienced secretaries and should know not to allow the phone to go unanswered. My question to them was "why should they know?" If the expectations have not been stated clearly, then the employee makes the assumption that it really doesn't matter. Fortunately, my husband took my advice and told Janice what he expected. As a result, Janice's performance improved.

Create a Supportive Climate

A positive Pygmalion establishes a climate or working environment in which people are comfortable, motivated, and enthusiastic. The boss (teacher or parent, for that matter) who attends to the positive nonverbal cues discussed in Strategy #8: Communication, will no doubt increase the likelihood of greater cooperation and improved results.

Strategy #7: Negotiation

*Remember not only to say the right thing at the right time
in the right place, but far more difficult still, to leave unsaid
the wrong thing at the wrong moment.*

Benjamin Franklin

We are faced every day with situations that require the use of
negotiation. We negotiate to resolve conflicts, solve problems, settle
differences of opinion, strengthen relationships, and develop a more
cooperative team (or even family) environment. Often we are unaware we are engaged in the negotiation process. Everyday events
such as where to go on vacation, with whose family we will spend
Thanksgiving, which child gets to use the car Saturday night, deciding a date for the next committee meeting, how a secretary's time is
to be divided among the three managers for whom she or he works,
can all be negotiated.

Honing your negotiation skills will improve your effectiveness as a manager and your interactions with coworkers or customers. You can even use it in your personal interactions with family members and friends.

Any situation where there is a conflict can be negotiated. Negotiation is a communication process in which the people involved consider alternatives in order to arrive at a mutually agreeable solution. During this process, the parties involved try to influence each other in order to satisfy their own needs.

Negotiation is not a contest - it is a strategy for influencing. It helps you feel more in charge or your life because you are being proactive rather than reactive resulting in a sense of personal and professional freedom. In a successful negotiation, everyone gains something. In order for us to understand the negotiation process, we must first explore the concept of conflict.

Understanding Conflict

"The truth is that for everything that can be accomplished by showing a person he is wrong, 10 times as much can be accomplished by showing him where he is right. The reason we don't do it is that it is more fun to throw a rock through a window than to put in a pane of glass."

Robert T. Allen

What is Conflict?

Simply stated, conflict occurs when the interests or concerns of two people are incompatible. Each person perceives his or her needs are being denied. When dealing with conflict, a person's behavior is defined along two dimensions: assertiveness, that is, the extent to which a person tries to satisfy his or her own concerns, and cooperation, the extent to which the individual attempts to satisfy the other person's concerns.

Disagreement is part of a conflict but is not the same as conflict. Two people may not be in agreement, that is, they may "see" things differently, but they don't necessarily believe their needs are being denied.

Principles and Assumptions

In trying to understand conflict, we must accept three givens: (1) conflict is inevitable; (2) conflict increases during times of change; and (3) conflict can be both positive and negative.

Negative Aspects

When we think of conflict, we tend to focus on the negative aspects. When left unmanaged, people pull apart, sometimes with disastrous results. In some cases, the conflict becomes so consuming that the people involved, directly or indirectly, can focus on nothing else, and their energy is diverted to dealing with nothing but the conflict. An atmosphere of tension, suspicion, and mistrust is created. The result is low morale and decreased productivity.

Positive Aspects

Although there are many negative outcomes associated with conflict, it can also be quite positive. First of all, conflicts provide us with an opportunity to learn more about ourselves and each other. Learning to communicate effectively to resolve conflict is a basic skill in all interpersonal relationships. Successful conflict resolution results in improved productivity and satisfying interpersonal interactions. Those who learn how to resolve conflict experience overall improved problem-solving abilities as they search for new approaches to existing problems. Successful conflict resolution helps the parties involved to clear the air and clarify issues. The result is improved communication and stronger relationships.

Symptoms of Conflict

Often conflict exists long before we recognize it. Sometimes it takes a major confrontation to bring the conflict to the surface. To help you diagnose and treat the "condition", be on the lookout for the following warning signs:

- *Lower productivity.* If you experience a change in others' or even your own productivity, stop and reflect on a possible reason. It just might be some type of conflict. Often when work output falls off, it's because people's energy is diverted elsewhere. They may have difficulty concentrating on their work, or the conflict may be resulting in uncooperative behavior. For example, a co-worker may decide to sabotage another's efforts by delaying or withholding information that the other person needs to do his or her job.

- *Tensions and arguments.* Dysfunctional and emotional behavior, such as shouting and slamming doors, is a sure sign that some type of conflict exists. People who lack the skills to resolve conflict will sometimes use physical means to express their anger or frustration. Often they do so to get someone's attention in hope that the other person will take some type of action.

- *Tardiness and absenteeism.* In some workplace situations, conflict can be so acute that people, either consciously or unconsciously, become more prone to illness (real or imagined) and call in "sick" or create situations that prevent them from getting to work on time. An increase in tardiness or absenteeism should alert the manager to a possible conflict situation.

- *Increased accidents and mistakes.* When people are caught up in emotional issues, they become distracted and are more likely to make mistakes and even cause or become involved in accidents.

- *Communication problems.* Examples of communication problems are endless, and many will be discussed in Strategy #8: Communication. One major symptom of a conflict, however, is when people actually stop communicating. When people avoid any interaction or begin communicating indirectly via memos, e-mail, or even through other people rather than meeting with or talking to each other directly, conflict may be the reason.

Similar to warning labels on medications, if any of these symptoms appear and persist beyond a reasonable time period, someone (preferably one or both of the parties involved) needs to address the situation. If not, then a third party (manager, family member, friend, etc.) needs to step in and either mediate the conflict or seek help in resolving it.

Causes of Conflict

In order to deal effectively with conflict, we must first identify the underlying causes. Unlike symptoms which are the signs or indicators that a conflict situation exists, causes are the underlying reasons or the situation that create the symptoms. Many conflicts are simply a result of differences. As we discussed in Strategy #5: Understanding, people need to develop their ability to understand and respect others' beliefs, values, and styles.

When we examine the causes of conflict, we cannot overlook ourselves. When a conflict exists, it's human nature for each person to blame the other. The first step should be to ask yourself, "To what degree have I contributed to the conflict?"

Many conflicts are simply a result of differences. As we discussed in Strategy #5: Understanding, people need to develop their ability to understand and respect others' beliefs, attitudes, and values. People are motivated by different needs and behavioral styles, and they all have different expectations.

One major source of conflict is the difference in perceptions. People simply interpret facts differently. Each person brings his or her unique perspective to the situation. This perspective is caused by differences in cultural backgrounds and life experiences. Based on a person's own psychological, emotional, or sociological position, he or she will focus on different aspects of the same event, situation, or issue.

As we will explore in detail in Strategy #8, communication problems abound in our society and are likely to continue to grow as we become more culturally diverse and more international in scope. Sometimes communication problems are related to the use of ambiguous words. Different groups tend to give common words special meanings. All you have to do is listen to a group of teenagers, and you'll get an idea of what I'm talking about. To many adults, these "kids" are speaking a foreign language, and in a sense, they are.

Preventing Conflict

It has been said that an ounce of prevention is worth a pound of cure. Conflict cannot be totally prevented, but it can be minimized. One of the major strategies for preventing conflict is good communication, which I will discuss in detail in Strategy #8.

Approaches to Conflict

There are a number of ways in which people approach or deal with conflict. The following are the five classic approaches. As you read each one, think about which one you tend to use most often:

Attack. The person who uses this approach goes on the offensive immediately. He or she is often aggressive and uncooperative and sees "the other side" as the enemy. The goal of the attacker is to win at all costs, satisfying his/her own needs at the expense of others. The attacker often uses formal authority, intimidation or majority rule. The result is hostility and resentment growing out of a win-lose situation. Since the attack approach takes less time, use it when there is no apparent effective resolution, in life-threatening situations, or with those who tend to take advantage.

Withdraw. At the other end of the spectrum is the person who withdraws. This person works hard to avoid any type of confrontation. He or she adopts the attitude that "It's just not worth it." In this approach, both parties lose because the conflict is not addressed, resulting in frustration and anger. Use when you do not have adequate information, if one or both parties needs time to cool down, or if the issue is relatively unimportant. One caveat: if too many problems are ignored or "swept under the rug" the result may be increased conflict.

Surrender. The outcome of the surrender approach is similar to that of the withdrawal. Although the other person wins, both parties lose. The person who surrenders is so eager to accommodate the other person that he or she places the other party's needs above his or her own. This "nice guy" approach allows others to take advantage. Use when it is important to maintain harmony and preserve the relationship. This approach can lead to the habit of giving in on all issues, resulting in a significant loss of one's power and reputation.

Bargain. On the surface, bargaining may seem to be the perfect answer to a conflict situation. With this approach, both people "sort of" win, and in some cases, that may be the best way of handling it. This approach is characterized by compromise and employs several negotiation techniques. This approach truly employs the give-get principle with both parties making a sacrifice to achieve a mutually workable solution, although neither side is really happy. Use when the problem is involved or complex and you must arrive at a resolution within a limited time frame.

Collaborate. If we take bargaining or compromise one step further, we reach collaboration, an outcome in which not only do I win and you win, but WE win because are working together toward a common goal. Collaboration takes time and major effort so that all parties are actively and equally involved in the process. In collaboration there is true cooperation. Success is defined in terms of gains, not losses. In a collaborative situation, people focus on goals and work to arrive at a win-win outcome using objective criteria. Collaboration seeks to satisfy needs and concerns of both parties. When those involved in the conflict help determine the solution, it is more likely they will support it.

Which style should I use? The appropriate style depends on the situation. Most people, however, develop one preferred style and use it in most situations. The goal is to be able to use any of the styles and know which is appropriate when.

Resolving Conflict

The first step in resolving conflict is to create an open and honest atmosphere. Keep in mind that you can disagree without being disagreeable. Also, as you work through the process, remember that you can't control the other person's behavior, only your own. You can, however, influence the other person through what you say and do.

R*equest feedback from team member(s).*
Create an appropriate climate for effective communication, including physical positioning. Seek additional information about the problem and ask for suggestions.

E*stablish a common goal.*
Focus on commonalities as a basis for resolving the conflict.

S*earch for areas of agreement.*
Concentrate on achieving two-way communication, and be persistent until you're sure you understand and are understood.

O*wn your anger and behavior.*
Ask yourself, "Who owns the problem?" In essence, both parties own the problem, but, once again, the only person whose behavior and emotions you can control is you. Begin by evaluating your own feelings. For example, anger, a common emotion in conflict situations, ranges from mild reactions ("I disagree") to medium responses ("I'm annoyed") to intense emotions ("I'm furious"). Learn to control your own anger. When dealing with another person's anger,

acknowledge the other person's emotion. Remember, feelings are neither right nor wrong - they just are.

Listen actively to clarify and confirm.
I have discussed active listening in detail in Strategy #4: Listening. Because it is such an important skill, however, one important point bears repeating. Clarify and confirm by stating what you understand the other person is saying and then asking if your understanding is correct.

Value and respect others' points of view.
Try to understand the other person's point of view, even though you do not agree with it. One way you can disagree without being disagreeable is to say, "I understand your position, but in my opinion..." or "I see it differently. I believe that..."

Express your thoughts and feelings unemotionally.
One way of getting and maintaining control is to engage in the practice of using "I statements", such as "I feel..." or "I believe..." "I statements" help level the playing field, so to speak. They help you express your beliefs or feelings without threatening, intimidating, or attacking the other person. In stating your position, it is important to describe the problem in terms of behavior, consequences, and feelings. Avoid drawing evaluative conclusions and attributing motives to the respondent. Expressing feelings is a little tricky, but stating your position calmly and objectively will help you achieve your desired outcome. For example, you might say, "I don't appreciate being told to... I would prefer that I be asked (my opinion, for my cooperation, etc.)."

The way in which you approach an interpersonal negotiating process is critical. Part of the planning process is to arm yourself with words and phrases that defuse the situation and create a sense of calm rather than confrontation. Be sure to include words like "we" and "us" to create a collaborate environment, such as "Let's talk this over so we can...."

Interpersonal Negotiating Process

Often we find ourselves in situations that require an actual negotiation process. A classic example in our personal lives, of course, is negotiating to buy a car. In a work-related situation, we might have to negotiate resources or deadlines, particularly in team-related or project management situations.

Planning and Preparation

The first step in the negotiation process is planning and preparation. We must have a strategy or plan of action. The following are a few of the things you might need to think about before you begin formal or even informal negotiation proceedings.

- **Know what you want.**

  It is critical to identify clearly for yourself what it is that you really want and what you are willing to give up, if necessary. Do you want more or less responsibility? Do you want to participate more in decisions? Do you want greater freedom or flexibility in your job? Do you want to change a procedure? Knowing what you want means identifying what you're willing to settle for or give up to get what you want, keeping in mind that we might have to give in order to get.

- **Assess your position**

  Part of the planning process is to analyze your position relative to what you want. What is your goal? How does it fit in to the "big picture"? How strong is your position, that is, how much power do you have? How much power does the other person have?

• **Gather information**

Never enter into a negotiation process without first doing your homework. This means gathering as much background information as you can about the situation and the people involved. Once again, this applies to both professional and personal situations. When I was about to lease a car for the first time, my husband and I (mostly my husband) spent hours reading about leases, both the benefits and the pitfalls. We read *Consumer Reports* and auto magazines. We asked friends about their experiences with various car dealers. By the time we were ready to begin visiting dealerships, I knew more about leases and cars than I ever cared to know, but in the end, all that research paid off. We were in a much stronger position to negotiate and although we didn't get exactly what we wanted, we were at least satisfied with the process.

• **Analyze the issues from both perspectives**

Although it is natural to approach a negotiation from our own perspective and self-interest, it is helpful to take the time to try to put ourselves in the shoes of the other person. What do we think the other person wants and why? What does he or she stand to gain or to lose? In the case of the car dealer, obviously profit is important. There may be, however, other secondary concerns as well, such as reputation.

Depending on what it is you are negotiating, the issue can become quite emotional. You can de-emotionalize the situation by brainstorming issues from the perspective of each party. How do you feel about the situation? Why do you feel so strongly about it? How do you think the other person feels? Why do you think he/she feels that way?

Before you enter into any negotiation situation, it is important that you maintain a high expectation for the outcome. It can become a self-fulfilling prophecy.

Doing the Negotiation

During the negotiation itself, you execute your strategy or plan of action by using various tactics following a step-by-step method. Throughout the negotiation process, practice good communication skills, i.e. questioning (close-ended and open-ended), observing (nonverbal cues such as facial, gestures, posture and sounds, clearing throat, etc.), active listening, etc.

- *Establish rapport.*

   Establish a cooperative climate. One way to begin is to choose neutral territory for your meeting. Sit on the same side of the desk or table, side by side. Establish the situation as a mutual problem. Begin using "we" statements, i.e. "How can *we* solve the problem?" or "Let's put *our* heads together to arrive at a workable solution."

- *Identify the issue, goals, objectives.*

   When you identify the issue, go beyond a simple statement of the problem. Include the effect of the problem as well as the personal impact of that effect. For example:

   "The decision to eliminate several positions (*problem statement*) has strongly affected my department. We are experiencing more absenteeism and less productivity (*effect statement*). This is causing me a great deal of stress and frustration (*feeling statement*)."

Next, focus on the common goal. We cannot assume that our goal and the other person's are the same. We must verify it by saying something like: "Our goal is to.... Do you agree?" If the person agrees, then move on. If not, there needs to be additional discussion until both parties can agree on the goal.

- **Relate your position.**

  Once you have agreement on the goal, then you need to state your position. You might use phrases similar to these:

  > "My position is that...."
  > "I thought it should be done this way. Let me explain my reasons for taking that approach."

- **Understand the other person's position.**

  After you have had an opportunity to state your position, then it's the other person's turn. Don't just pacify or placate the other party by allowing him or her to be heard. Really try to understand where he or she "is coming from." Here's where active listening techniques can be quite helpful:

  > "Let me try to understand your position. As I understand it, you.... Is that right?"

- **Identify areas of agreement.**

  Stress your desire to resolve the issue by restating each position as you see it and suggesting that you start by working with areas of agreement. The statement might sound something like this:

  > "I can see merit in your position, although I don't agree with it. I do agree that... but I disagree that....

I would like to suggest that we start with those things on which we can agree and go from there."

- **Identify barriers to agreement.**

Of course, there are areas where you do not agree; therefore, the next step is to identify the barriers to agreement. Again, we cannot assume the other person sees it the same way. To ensure that both parties recognize the same barriers, you might try the following approach:

"As I see it, what is getting in the way is.... Is that also how you perceive the situation?"

- **Brainstorm solutions and alternatives.**

Once you have gotten agreement on where you agree and disagree, then brainstorm solutions and alternatives. Get creative. Generate and evaluate possible solutions. Reassess your positions and evaluate each proposed solution, always with the common goal in mind:

"Let's take a look at some possible alternative...."
"What if...."

- **Get agreement.**

Finally, decide on the best solution together. Plan the implementation of the solution, responsibilities of each party along with how and when. Then plan a follow-up so that both parties can evaluate the solution.

Avoiding Mistakes

Negotiation often fails because those involved fail to manage the process. The following are some tips to help you avoid common pitfalls:

- **Inadequate preparation**

  As mentioned earlier, preparation is key. Find out as much as you can before you meet with the other person(s). Mentally prepare by thinking about and even writing down what you are going to say and anticipating what the other person might say.

- **Impatience**

  Conflict resolution and negotiation take time. In our "quick fix" society, people are often unwilling to spend the time and effort to arrive at an amicable resolution to a problem or disagreement. Be willing to do whatever it takes to create a win-win situation.

- **Aggressive behavior - arguing, trying to intimidate, losing temper**

  We are human beings with many emotions. The important thing is to keep those emotions under control. Don't risk "winning the battle, but losing the war." Aggressive behavior may work in the short term, but for lasting results, seek to arrive at a win-win outcome.

- **Insisting on getting own way, ignoring give/get principle**

  Only spoiled, willful children insist on getting their own way. Mature adults, on the other hand, recognize that life is a series of compromises and that sometimes we have to give in order to get. Keep in mind, however, that the most effective approach is collaboration.

- **Poor communication skills - talking too much, not listening**

  Once again, communication skills are critical. Don't interrupt the other person, but by the same token, don't allow yourself to be interrupted. People are much more receptive if they believe they are being listened to. To be a successful negotiator, practice active listening throughout the process.

Remember that negotiation takes time, skill, energy, and patience. But the pay-off is well worth the effort.

Strategy #8: Communication

No visual image is as vivid as the image created by the mind in response to words... The ability to throw a loop around human personality and penetrate the inner space of character is exceeded by nothing that can be given visual form.

Norman Cousins

Communication is the most fundamental, complex, and critical human interaction. It is the basis for and an integral part of each of the other eight strategies discussed in this book.

In this chapter, we will focus on your role as the initiator in the communication process and how you can fine-tune this skill to influence others in any situation.

Modes of Communication

In his book *Silent Messages* published in 1971, Professor Albert Mehrabian of UCLA shares the results of his study dealing with the relationship among the three elements present every time we speak. According to Mehrabian, each communication is a transaction made up of the following:

- Verbal   - what we say
- Vocal   - how we say it
- Visual   - how we show it

In order for us to be believable, there must be consistency among these three elements. Interestingly, the element that has the greatest influence is visual with 55%, followed by vocal (38%). What we actually say (verbal) accounts for only 7%!

Communication is more than the process of the sender, receiver, message, and channel. Far more complex, it is really eight communications in one. We start with what we mean to say (part 1) versus what we actually say (part 2). How many times have you said "That's not what I meant" because what came out of your mouth was not what was in your head? This is then followed by what the other person hears (part 3) and is assigned meaning based on what the receiver thinks he or she hears (part 4). This process becomes complicated even further by what the other person means to respond (part 5) and what he or she actually says (part 6). Completing the communication loop is what we hear the other person say (part 7) and what we think we hear (part 8).

Barriers to Effective Communication

Emotions

Einstein once said that "Although words exist for the most part for the transmission of ideas, there are some which produce such violent disturbance in our feelings that the role they play in the transmission of ideas is lost in the background."

Making Assumptions

One of the biggest mistakes each of us makes in our daily verbal interactions with others is that we hear what the person says and then *assume* we know what he or she means without really "checking it out."

Poor Listening

Because we have discussed listening in Strategy #4, we only need to reiterate that poor listening habits often rob us of clear communication and result in misunderstandings that can have a far-reaching impact both personally and professionally.

Semantics

Words, phrases, and statements mean different things to different people. This is particularly significant in our diverse, multi-cultural society. We could devote an entire chapter to the discussion of semantics among different cultures or even geographic regions within the United States. While people may be aware of those obvious and significant differences, many overlook the everyday casual use and different interpretations of common words and phrases. For example, how often do you use the phrase *as soon as possible*? What does it really mean? In many of my workshops, I ask participants to write down the particular time frame they associate with the phrase *as soon as possible*. They must give it a specific number and time frame in terms of minutes, hours, days, weeks, and so forth such as five minutes, three hours, two days, or one week. I then ask each person to tell us what he or she put down. The results are quite revealing. I have had responses in the same group ranging from one minute to two weeks. Think about the implication of those responses. The point, of course, is that words mean different things to different people because each of us has a different frame of reference, and those differences can have a major impact on our interactions and relationships with others. In one situation, I was working with a twelve-person management team of a small organization. In the exercise, the Chief Operating Officer's interpretation was twenty-four hours. The reaction of her direct reports was both surprise and relief. As one of her managers put it, "All this time when you said 'as soon as possible' we thought you meant for us to drop everything and do what you wanted immediately. Now we find out the next day would be okay." This was just one indication of the major morale and communication problems that plagued the organization. Once we began to address the need to be specific, the communication improved considerably.

I also ask people to assign a percentage to the word "usually" and find that the responses range from 15% to 95%. Again, consider the difference in interpretation when, for example, a manager is evaluating an employee's performance and remarks that the employee "usually" completes his or her work on time. This whole issue of semantics reminds me of a "Family Circus" cartoon which shows the mother with the front door open and her child with many friends waiting to come in. The caption reads: "You said I could bring some friends home, but I don't know how many some is."

Along the same line, in Lily Tomlin's play *The Search for Signs of Intelligent Life in the Universe*, written by Jane Wagner, the character Bag Lady Trudy talks about her imaginary "space chums." She has the following conversation with herself: "I could kick myself. I told 'em I'd meet 'em on the corner of 'Walk, Don't Walk' 'round lunchtime. Do they even know what 'lunch' means? I doubt it. And 'round'. Why did I say 'round'? Why wasn't I more specific?"

The need to be clear and specific also applies to family situations as well. A parent may tell a teenage child to come home early from a party making the assumption that "early" to the parent may be eleven o'clock, whereas the child's interpretation may be totally different. Many family arguments could be avoided if all parties involved assign the same meaning to the same word(s). The lesson here is to be as specific as possible, communicating clearly desired time frames, amounts, percentages, and numbers.

Vocabulary and Word Choices

We can influence people either positively or negatively by the words we choose to use in expressing our thoughts, ideas, or opinions. Keep in mind that the word is not the thing. Rather it is a symbol to represent the thing or concept. Because words mean different things to different people, and in fact, mean different things to the same person at different times, we can never really communicate to another person exactly what we think or feel. We can, however, come close by choosing our words carefully. As Mark Twain once said, "The difference between the *almost*-right word and the *right* word is really a large matter - it's the difference between the lightning bug and the lightning."

Style Differences

As we explored in detail in Strategy #5: Understanding, people have many different styles. We have different learning styles, personality styles, communication styles, leadership styles, and so forth. These style differences frequently get in the way of effective communication. It's almost as though two people are speaking a different language. To increase our effectiveness, we must recognize these style differences and adjust accordingly.

Verbal: Delivering Your Message

Communicating Orally

We've all heard, "It's not what you say but how you say it." While it's true that your tone of voice and body language impact meaning and communicate volumes, often sending mixed signals, what we say is extremely important. Words are powerful. They can hurt or they can help. In either case, we influence and are influenced by words. If you have any doubts, just read the headlines or listen to the news. Many a politician has been hurt and careers ruined because of poor word choices. During the Bush administration, Vice President Dan Quayle became the brunt of many jokes because he sometimes inadvertently misstated a thought or idea.

As colleagues, parents, and friends we often use words and phrases that either encourage or discourage, often without knowing the result or outcome of our remarks.

Look at the following "discourager" phrases and check those you might be guilty of using:

- *Yes, but...*
- *We've tried that before and...*
- *What you mean is...*
- *Let's discuss it some other time...*
- *You haven't considered...*
- *You have to...*

- *You're obviously confused..*
- *I don't have time right now...*
- *It's not in the budget...*
- *Why did you...*
- *That's a dumb idea...*
- *You don't understand...*
- *You're wrong about...*

How did you do? Many of us are unaware of the impact of these phrases and others like them on other people. You might be thinking about now, "Well, I may use these phrases sometimes, but I really don't mean them to be negative." That may be true; however, the next time you're tempted to use a "discourager" phrase, ask yourself the following questions: What is my intent? How am I (or would I be) perceived? Remember, perception is reality.

Read the list below and notice how much more positive and encouraging these phrases are. Think about the impact of this list versus the list above.

- *That's an interesting point...*
- *I appreciate your hard work...*
- *I never thought of that...*
- *Good job!*
- *I have faith in you...*
- *I know you can do it...*
- *Give it a try...*
- *You're on the right track....*

Can you think of others to add to either list? If you find yourself using any of the "discourager" phrases, reword the phrase to be more encouraging and positive.

Using "I Messages"

"I messages" are statements designed to give the receiver feedback about his or her behavior. As I discussed in Strategy #3, the use of "I messages" promotes open communication. "I messages" are very effective in reducing the other person's defensiveness and resistance to further communication. The responsibility lies with the sender who delivers the message honestly, expressing feelings, focusing on behavior description, not evaluation. On the other hand, "you messages" blame, accuse, or attack the other person, causing him or her to respond emotionally and negatively. Because an "I message" communicates how the sender experiences the other person's behavior, the receiver is more likely to accept the sender's comments as positive feedback. As a result, the receiver will respond more positively.

Interaction Analysis

One way in which we can look at our interactions with others is through Interaction Analysis, developed by Ned Flanders at the University of Minnesota in the early 1960s. Interaction Analysis is a system for examining and understanding verbal interactions. It helps us identify and choose constructive ways to talk to and interact with others. Flanders identifies two types of "talk" or verbal behaviors that are used to influence others: indirect and direct. Research shows that indirect verbal behaviors are the most effective in influencing others, yet most of us spend our time and efforts using direct talk. Indirect is more effective because it expands the freedom of other people to participate whereas direct influencing behavior restricts freedom and stifles individual response. On the other hand, indirect encourages initiative, independence, and self-expression and creates a collaborative atmosphere.

The person who uses indirect influence practices four verbal behaviors. First, and perhaps the most difficult, is *accepts feelings*. When we make statements such as "I can imagine that what he said upset you," we are accepting feelings. For the most part, society in the United States does not encourage an expression of feelings, particularly in the business world. If feelings are expressed or acknowledged, they are generally negative. The following is an example of "talk" that accepts feelings:

Employee:	"Senior management has no idea what it's like to have a customer yelling at you when you're just trying to do your job."
Manager:	"It's stressful and frustrating when you're caught in the middle between company policy and satisfying the customer."

The second indirect category is *praises or encourages*. This may be expressed verbally or nonverbally. Nodding the head or saying "go on" encourages the other person to elaborate or expand on his or her point. The "encourager" phrases mentioned earlier are good examples of praise and encouragement. Think about the powerful positive impact a statement like, "I know you can do it" will have on a person.

Another challenging indirect verbal category is *accepts or uses ideas*. In this category, we clarify, build, and develop ideas that were just mentioned or suggested by the other person. This technique is similar to that used in active listening. When you respond to someone by saying, "Let me make sure I understand what you're saying. As I hear it, you're saying that..."

The final indirect category and seemingly the easiest is *asks questions*. The key here is to ask broad open-ended questions designed to elicit a more thorough and thoughtful response from the other person. Questions that begin with "who," "what," "when," "where," and "how" encourage the other person to explain his or her thoughts more thoroughly or completely.

As mentioned earlier, the most frequently used and least effective "talk" is direct. The most common category is *gives information*. Parents and managers are particularly good at giving facts, expressing their own ideas or opinions, and asking rhetorical questions.

Even more restrictive is that of *gives directions*. Once again, those in positions of authority take full advantage of telling others where, when, and how to do something.

Finally, *criticizes or justifies authority* is behavior in which the individual uses "discourager" phrases and engages in "put downs." Statements such as "I can't believe you made such a simple mistake" is sure to cause the other person to "shut down" thus limiting any further communication.

Mirroring and Pacing

A very effective way to build trust and rapport is through mirroring and pacing. Much of the study in this area (called neurolinguistic programming) was done in the mid-1970s by John Grinder and Richard Bandler. According to studies, people describe their experiences in one of three representation systems: visual (sight), auditory (sound), or kinesthetic (feelings). Good communicators listen carefully for the representational systems and use that knowledge to understand how another person communicates and then matches or mirrors that behavior both verbally and nonverbally. The other person will have a greater understanding and acceptance if the message is in accordance with his or her dominant representation system as illustrated in the following three sentences:

"Does this *look* like it will get the job done?"
"Does it *sound* like it will get the job done?"
"Do you *feel* that it will get the job done?"

Those who are visual want to see pictures, charts, graphs, or be given a broad overview, that is, the "big picture." Auditory people, on the other hand, want facts and details and enjoy listening. Finally, people who are kinesthetic enjoy completing questionnaires and engaging in activities such as group discussions.

First of all, you must be aware of the types of words that fall into each representational system and be aware of your own preference. For example, which of the following are you most likely to say:

"I *see* what you're saying."   Visual
"I *hear* what you're saying."   Auditory
"I *catch* what you're saying." Kinesthetic

When we talk about mirroring, we suggest that we adjust to rather than exactly match the other person's voice tone, tempo, volume, and words. This process also encourages the speaker to note and repeat in his or her own language the primary verbs the other person uses. Further nonverbal mirroring involves matching breathing rate to that of the other person as well as posture and body movements.

Some people may use several modalities rather than one preferred way of processing and organizing information. We can influence others by communicating in the other person's preferred modality. How do you identify an individual's preferred modality? You must carefully *listen* (Strategy #4) and *watch*. Have you even been involved in a discussion with someone who brings out a scrap of paper, napkin, placemat, etc. and draws a picture or diagram? It's a safe bet that person is visual. The visual person will tend to say "Let me see" or "I get the picture." The auditory person will spend time listening to educational tapes and uses phrases such as "That rings a bell" or "That sounds about right." The kinesthetic person likes to discuss, debate, engage in multiple activities at the same time (e.g. opening the mail while talking on the telephone), and in conversation, may say something like, "I need to get a handle on this."

Giving Directions

How many times in both your personal and professional life have you given someone directions? You may have given someone directions to your house or simply told a person what you wanted him or her to do. Then when the other person doesn't do it "right", that is, according to your expectations, you naturally blame the other person for not listening. Remember the "paper-tearing" exercise discussed in Strategy #4? Always keep in mind that what may be perfectly clear to us is not always clear to the other person. Although giving directions should be a two-way process, the onus is on the sender of information to make sure what he or she meant is what is actually received and understood. Someone once said, "I know you believe you understand what you think I just said, but I'm not sure you realize that what you heard is not what I meant."

First and foremost, directions and requests should be reasonable and made in a polite tone rather than that of a drill sergeant barking orders. Secondly, make sure that your directions are understandable by being specific, setting time limits and standards of performance whenever possible. Finally, ask for feedback to ensure the other person understands what you want.

Communicating on Paper

Not only do we need to be careful of what we say face to face, but we also need to be mindful of how we come across on paper. Corporate America is awash in a sea of interoffice memos that degrade, demoralize, and anger employees. The following memo is a case in point:

To: *All Employees*
From: *Human Resources*
Date: *December 1, 19-*
Subject: *Policy Change: Workplace Eating*

Effective immediately, employees will no longer be permitted to consume any food or beverages at your desks or work stations. This policy is necessary to prevent any further costs to the organization. Violation of the policy will not be tolerated. There will be no exceptions!

How would you feel if you received such a memo? Angry? Insulted? Notice the negative tone created by "no longer permitted" and "will not be tolerated." Compare this memo with the following:

To: *All Employees*
From: *Human Resources*
Date: *December 1, 19-*
Subject: *Policy Change: Workplace Eating*

We have recently experienced a substantial increase in costs to repair and replace computers and other equipment damaged by spilled beverages in work areas. We have also been experiencing an increase in unwanted "varmints" attracted by food crumbs and leftovers around the office. As a result, we are asking you to help us avoid further costs and unsanitary conditions by using only the lunch room and other designated "break" areas to enjoy your snacks and beverages. We realize this is an inconvenience and, therefore, we are adding five additional minutes to each official "break." We also realize that many departments have already made plans for holiday celebrations, and in keeping with the holiday spirit, our new policy will take effect January 1.

We thank you for your cooperation in helping us maintain a safe and healthy work environment for everyone.

Notice the difference in tone. First of all, the approach establishes a cooperative relationship. It communicates that "we're in this together." Secondly, the approach is adult to adult as opposed to the parent-child relationship implied in the first example. Thirdly, the memo gives a reason for the new policy, and finally, the memo communicates empathy, understanding, and respect for the employees by not interfering with the holiday festivities and expanding the "break" period to accommodate the inconvenience. Which memo would you rather receive?

Vocal

If you're serious about improving your vocal image, take every opportunity to tape yourself. Listen to yourself on tape and note what you like and don't like about the way you sound. Use the following categories to assess yourself as objectively as possible. In addition to your self-assessment, ask a family member or close friend to critique you as well. You may even want to consider hiring a speech coach to help you identify "speech blemishes" and take you through exercises to improve those areas that may be hindering your effectiveness.

Tone

Tone has to do with the quality of your voice and may be described with words such as *shrill, nasal, hoarse,* or *rasping.* Tone refers to the quality of sound, including intonation that expresses a feeling such as irritation, sadness, frustration, anger, or joy. The tone of your voice changes to reflect the emotions you are experiencing, and for that reason, is often difficult to control.

Volume

Volume, of course, refers to the loudness or softness with which a person speaks. If people are frequently asking you to repeat what you just said, that may be an indication that you are speaking too softly. Concentrate on speaking up. On the other hand, it is possible to speak too loudly. If your friends and family members admonish you to "tone it down" you might need to work on lowering your voice.

Tempo

Tempo is the rate at which one speaks. If you speak too fast, listeners will have difficulty understanding you. If you speak too slowly, they'll get bored and may stop listening altogether. Acceptable speaking rates are between 120 and 160 words per minute. You do, however, want to provide variety by changing your speed, speeding up, slowing down, or even pausing, to emphasize points and maintain audience interest.

Enunciation/Pronunciation

Articulation is the precision and clarity with which a person speaks and includes both enunciation and pronunciation. Enunciation is the full and distinct utterance of syllables. Pronunciation, on the other hand, refers to the correct way the word should be said, including appropriate emphasis on the syllables and the use of the long or short vowel sound. To be an effective communicator, it is important to pronounce words correctly and enunciate them clearly.

Accents

An accent refers to the unique speech patterns, including inflections and intonations, characteristic of a particular group or locale. Accents can be distracting and get in the way of effective communication. Many individuals spend a great deal of money and time working with an accent-reduction coach to improve diction and "neutralize" their speech patterns.

Visual: The Nonverbal Agenda

Although, to some degree, we have already dealt with visual in our discussion of image, our first strategy, I would like to address more specifically the science of nonverbal communication or kinesis. The following are just a few of the body language techniques that you can use not only to reinforce your verbal communication but also to help you "read" others more accurately and thus improve your interpersonal interaction.

In fact, nonverbal communication including gestures, pauses, and body movements are indicators of conflicts that may not be readily apparent through verbal communication.

Gestures

- Open, relaxed hands with palms turned upward communicate sincerity and openness.

- Hands together in prayer-like fashion, sometimes referred to as stippling, are a display of self-confidence.

- Tugging at your ear says that you are anxious to participate.

- Playing with pens, eye glasses, paper clips, rubber bands, etc. is a sign of impatience, boredom, or nervousness.

- Partially covering your mouth when you talk is an indication of uncertainty or self-doubt.

Posture and Body Movement

- Leaning back with hands behind head and stretching is a demonstration of superiority.

- Arms crossed in front indicates defensiveness.

- Removing glasses and putting the ear piece in your mouth is used when we want to pause for thought or delay giving an answer.

- Clenched fists are a pretty good indication of anger.

- Sitting on the edge of the chair shows that the person is interested and ready to interact.

- In contrast, sitting with one leg over the arm of a chair is a sign of indifference or uninvolvement.

- Wringing one's hands shows insecurity.

- Fidgeting in the chair is an indication of either nervousness or discomfort.

Facial Expressions and Eye Contact

- Avoiding eye contact suggests that the person wants to limit the interaction.

- Raised eyebrows show surprise or questioning of what has just been said.

- A sideways glance communicates doubt, suspicion, and mistrust.

Distancing and Touching

Space or distance (proxemics) is an important factor in nonverbal communication. The issue of personal space or distance varies from one culture to another. I once had an employee who made me very uncomfortable each time we stood talking one on one. It took me a long time to figure out why I was so uncomfortable in her presence; finally I realized that she violated "my space" each time we spoke. She always stood *very* close to me, almost nose to nose, and when I stepped back to get some distance, she would move toward me to narrow the distance. I found myself avoiding one-on-one discussions with her. When I began to study and learn more about body language, I discovered the reason for my discomfort. In Western society, we have very specific zones appropriate for specific people and situations. For example, our *intimate* zone, reserved for family and very close friends is sixteen to eighteen inches. Our *personal* zone, one and one-half to four feet, is observed in social functions with casual friends and acquaintances. The phrase "keeping someone at arm's length" now begins to make sense. We have a *social* zone of four to twelve feet for strangers and a *public* zone of twelve feet or more when we are addressing large groups.

Subvocal

- Clearing one's throat suggests that the individual may be uncertain.

- A grunt-like noise shows disapproval or displeasure.

- "Uh" and "um" are often signals that the person is unsure of himself/herself.

Symbolic Communication

Whether we like it or not, our clothing, personal artifacts, and other material items play a big part in influencing others. As we noted in Strategy #1: Image, the role of material items in creating an image is significant. Our appearance, including clothing, hair, cosmetics and make-up, jewelry as well as the car we drive, the house and neighborhood we live in, and our office or work area send a message, either positive or negative, to those we want to influence.

Each of us has certain expectations about what someone in a particular profession or position should "look like." Any deviation from that image has the potential for disastrous results. When you hear the word "banker" you probably think of someone dressed in a conservative dark suit with appropriately matched accessories. Even the banker, however, needs to be mindful of his or her customers and adjust accordingly. The loan officer calling on a farmer may have a better chance of influencing and landing the business if he or she dresses more casually.

Response Modes

The way in which we respond to people communicates acceptance or nonacceptance. When we use nonaccepting response modes, many of which were mentioned earlier in this chapter as "discourager" phrases, we devalue others and cause them to become resistant. Often we are unaware that we use these nonaccepting behaviors and their impact on others. How many times do we find ourselves in the warning mode with statements such as, "If you don't..."? And what about the sermonizing effect of unsolicited advice when we say, "You ought to..." or "If I were you, I would..."? Along these same lines, we sometimes and inadvertently assume the role of diagnostician with statements such as, "What you need is...." Consider how it feels when someone challenges or questions you by asking, "Why did you...?" Ask yourself if you are ever guilty of "putting down" others by saying, "You think you have it bad... when that happened to me..." or the patronizing effect of "You'll get over it..." or "You'll be okay..." Finally, think about the devaluing message of "You shouldn't feel that way...." Always remember that what you intend may not be what the other person hears.

Improving Communication

Use the following checklist to identify the action items you want to adopt to become a more effective communicator:

- *Create a climate that encourages open communication.* Use body language that says, "I want to listen to you." Smile when you speak and allow your natural warmth and charm to show through.

- *Be clear and concise when delivering your message.* Organize your thoughts before "putting your mouth in gear." Then speak distinctly and clearly using the appropriate volume and tempo.

- *Be sensitive to others.* Demonstrate empathy, concern, and support. Refrain from being accusing or judgmental.

- *Communicate in the other person's style, not yours.* Be aware of your own communication style and its effect on others. Practice adjusting your style to the situation and the other person in order to connect and be understood.

- *Practice active listening.* Reflect and play back what the other person is saying, thinking, or feeling.

- *Seek out others' feelings and thoughts.* Ask open-ended questions and then practice other indirect verbal behaviors such as "uh-huh" and "You sound concerned."

- *Show interest and attentiveness through eye contact, active listening, and mirroring techniques.* Observe the other person carefully and encourage further communication by clarifying and confirming what you think you heard and choosing words and nonverbal behaviors that allow you to connect with the other person.

- *Use effective feedback.* Concentrate on using "I messages" to communicate how the person's behavior is making you feel and its impact on you.

Communication is the key to and the fundamental building block for all the other influencing strategies. We all must be able to communicate effectively to those around us if we are to experience professional and personal success.

Strategy #9: Empowerment

Never tell people how to do things. Tell them what to do and they will surprise you with their ingenuity.

George Patton

What is Empowerment?

Empowerment is the buzz word of the '90s. We hear it used both in business and in personal situations. What does it really mean? Empowerment means making people feel valued by involving them in decisions, incorporating their ideas, asking them to participate in the planning process, praising them, and recognizing and rewarding them for their achievements and efforts.

Empowerment works. In corporations across the United States, self-directed work teams meet regularly to brainstorm ways to save money and work more efficiently.

People are thinking beings. They make important decisions every day in their personal lives, yet employers often expect them to leave their brains at the door when they come to work.

Personal Empowerment

In order to empower others, we must begin by empowering ourselves. How often have you felt you lost control of a situation? How did that make you feel? Feeling a loss of power and control creates low self-esteem which in turn affects our performance and how we interact with others. We must engage in self-directed, that is, assertive, behavior. Since personal empowerment has its roots in assertiveness skills training, let's start by defining the various behaviors that frame our interactions with others: assertive, aggressive, passive, passive-aggressive.

Before I share my definitions with you, I would like you to complete an exercise I often ask of participants in my "Art of Influencing" workshop. Think about and identify three people, real or fictional, dead or alive, that you would label "assertive." Then develop a composite list of qualities, characteristics, and behaviors they exhibit that caused you to identify them as assertive people.

Whom did you choose? Frequently, participants list historical figures such as Hitler or Napoleon and television characters like Roseanne and Murphy Brown. Sometimes they cite media celebrities like Rush Limbaugh and Howard Stern. The qualities, characteristics, and behaviors they list often include words such as bold, outspoken, blunt, forceful, aggressive, domineering.

I then offer a definition of assertiveness and ask them to evaluate their choices of people and descriptors in light of the definition. They quickly discover, like most people, that they have equated assertiveness with aggressiveness.

Assertive Behavior

Assertiveness means expressing your thoughts, needs, and feelings directly and honestly without violating the rights of others. Assertive individuals are direct, honest, firm, tactful, positive, and confident. Assertive people listen attentively while allowing others to express their feelings. They maintain direct eye contact, have an erect, relaxed posture and speak their mind openly and directly with words such as "Let's...", "We could...", "I want [need, expect, would like, would prefer]."

Example: *I would like some help with the dishes.*

One word of caution: any strength taken to an extreme becomes a weakness or liability. Notice the extremes and their result in the descriptions of aggressive, passive, and passive-aggressive behaviors.

Aggressive Behavior

Aggressive behavior is any action that disregards the rights and feelings of others. When people become too direct or focus too much on themselves and their own needs, they demonstrate aggressive behavior by putting others down, intimidating, becoming stubborn, rude, and insensitive. Their posture is rigid with hands on hips and feet apart, gesturing with clenched fists or finger-pointing. Aggressive people blame, accuse, attack, and demand. Their statements start with "You did...," "You'd better...", "You should...", "You must be kidding...."

Example: *Could you could get off your lazy rear long enough to help me clean up?*

Aggressive people are bold, forceful, pushy, domineering, insensitive, and belligerent. The result is that the other person is resentful, less cooperative, defensive, demotivated, angry or hurt, and less productive.

Passive Behavior

Passive or avoidant behavior is described as weak or "wishy-washy." Passive individuals act indirectly and avoid any type of confrontation. Passive people are overly sensitive and indirect; they allow others to control them, and they often hold feelings inside or express them indirectly. Their voice tone is frequently weak, hesitant, and soft. Their eyes are downcast with their posture characterized by hunched shoulders. Using fidgety, distracting, or nervous gestures, passive people qualify, apologize, and question: "Is it okay...?" "Do you mind if...," "Could I...?", "Would you mind very much...", "I guess...", "Don't bother...."

Example: *I wonder if you could help with the dishes.*

Passive behavior results in unresolved problems, frustration, stress, confusion, and poor performance.

Passive-Aggressive Behavior

Passive-aggressive behavior is devious and hurtful to others. Passive-aggressive or manipulative people make others look bad or feel guilty, often using sarcasm to make a point. They engage in deception, gossip, and uncooperative behavior and take advantage of others in indirect, subtle ways. Passive-aggressive people shift their bodies and avoid direct eye contact with sideways glances instead.

Example: *Even though I have put in a very long and difficult day at the office and rushed home to fix you a nice meal, I'll do the dishes myself so you can rest.*

The result of such manipulative behavior is distrust, resentment, hurt, and poor performance.

Barriers to Acting Assertively

If assertive behavior is so positive, why do we find it so difficult? What gets in the way of our being more assertive? The major barrier is our own inner voice grounded in many of the messages we heard growing up:

- *People won't like me.*
- *People will think I'm pushy.*
- *I'm afraid I'll hurt someone's feelings.*
- *People will think I'm selfish.*

Think about situations in which you would like to be more assertive, but remember that being assertive allows you to choose not to be assertive. In some situations, you may decide that the better course of action is to be passive, aggressive, or even passive-aggressive. The choice is yours. That's personal empowerment. Knowing how and when to be assertive can help improve both personal and professional relationships.

Distinguishing Behaviors

To find out how well you understand the differences among the four types of behavior, read the following interpersonal situations and indicate if the situation is assertive (AS), aggressive (AG), passive (P), or passive-aggressive (PA).

1. You are in a meeting with your peers, and your boss tells you to take the minutes. You resent doing so because you have done it for the last three meetings and believe others should take their turn. You respond by saying, "I have taken the minutes for the last three meetings. In order to be fair, I suggest we take turns, starting with this meeting."

2. At a meeting, a co-worker often interrupts you when you are speaking and when you offer an idea or suggestion, he questions whether or not it will work. You react by saying, "Look, I'm getting tired of your interruptions and criticisms. At least I have ideas. That's more than I can say for you."

3. Because you often work on weekends, you have no time to schedule personal appointments. In fact, you have put off a long-overdue visit to the dentist. You finally decided that you can no longer put this off, and you approach your boss by saying, "I really hate to ask you, but I have really been putting in a lot of hours, and I need to make an appointment to see my dentist. Would it be okay if I leave a few minutes early one day next week?"

4. You pride yourself on getting along with everyone, and you are always willing to go out of your way to help someone else. There is one person, however, who you find to be annoying and even abrasive. She is extremely

rude and demanding when she calls on the telephone. When you answer the phone, she abruptly says, "I have questions for you" or "You have to give me this information." As a result you now go out of your way to avoid her phone calls or when you do talk to her, you tell her you will get the information for her and then "conveniently" forget to do it. When she calls to follow up, you apologize and tell her that you have been so overwhelmed with work that you haven't had a chance to get to it, but you'll do it just as soon as you can.

Answers: 1-AS; 2-AG; 3-P; 4-PA

Remember that assertiveness involves:

- Knowing yourself and what you need.

- Communicating your need.

- Respecting others.

- Choosing the most appropriate action for a particular situation.

Involving Others

We empower others by creating an environment where people are encouraged to explore, discover, take risks, and develop mutual trust. We enable others to succeed by providing them with the means, opportunity, and capacity they need to excel. The result is growth, innovation, and satisfaction. People feel important and a part of the whole whether it is an organization, community, or family. To quote an ancient Chinese proverb, "Give a man a fish and you feed him for a day. Teach a man to fish and you feed him for a lifetime." They feel competent and confident in their abilities. Those who practice empowerment are comfortable sharing authority, control, responsibility, and rewards.

People who are empowered feel they have some control over themselves and those things for which they are accountable. They feel they have some say in how things are done and that what they say and think actually matters, whether it be an employee involved in a process improvement effort or a child consulted on how he or she would like his or her room decorated. An empowered employee feels he/she is being treated as an adult, and, as a result, the employee will rise to the occasion and do the best job possible. An empowered child will learn responsibility and self-confidence which leads to increased self-esteem, a critical factor for future success.

In a corporate environment, successful companies are those that believe and practice employee empowerment. They have no choice if they want to compete in the global marketplace.

Empowerment is good for business. In a January 1996 article in *The Philadelphia Inquirer,* Sears chairman Arthur Martinez is quoted as saying that "a decision made in favor of the customer on the floor at the point of contact is a decision made in favor of the store."

The Seattle-based Nordstrom chain is noted for its unwavering commitment to serving the customer. Sales associates are able to deliver what amounts to "legendary" service because they are empowered to do so. The Nordstrom philosophy allows employees to think, to use their judgment, and to make decisions. The half-page employee handbook affirms simply that the number one goal is to provide superior customer service, that employees should set high goals, and that the organization has confidence the employees will achieve them. Furthermore, the statement encourages each employee to use his or her "good judgment in all situations."

Empowerment must be genuine. Often managers, teachers, parents, and others in power positions tout empowerment and extol its virtues but, in practice, are reluctant to give away control. The result is false empowerment as a result of incongruence as we looked at in Strategy #1. A prime example of false empowerment is America's public schools. Teachers and administrators preach personal responsibility, individual accountability, and creative thinking. They profess their commitment to developing students to think for themselves and explore options and possibilities, yet the system of rules with rigid do's and don'ts is anything but empowering. They want students to care about the school and treat school property with respect, yet rarely are students included in decisions that affect them. In many cases, teachers and parents don't fare much better. Important decision-making responsibility is closely held by administrators. The same is true in both corporations and households across the country.

Children who are not allowed to have a say in those decisions that affect them can hardly be expected to behave like adults when they reach the magical age of eighteen.

Understanding Motivation

Can you motivate someone? The answer is an emphatic, "NO". Motivation is something that comes from within the individual to prompt or incite an action. Motivation is a function of individual will. We do things because the outcome is appealing to us and serves as an incentive.

People are motivated by unmet needs, and those needs differ from individual to individual. People's needs are determined by their unique set of circumstances, their value and belief systems, family background, education, work experience, and their individual personality styles.

Motivation is directly related to morale, that is, the attitude of individuals and groups toward their work, environment, and organization as a whole. Morale affects employee performance which, in turn, affects organizational results.

Assessing Your Approach

If you are a manager, you may find yourself puzzled by an employee's apparent lack of motivation. You pay a decent salary and don't understand why this person isn't grateful just to have a job. The first step to real understanding is to accept the fact that what motivates you may or may not motivate your employees. Take a moment and rank order the following motivating factors according to what is important to you:

- Full appreciation of work done

- Feeling of being in on things

- Sympathetic help on personal problems

- Job security

- Good wages

- Interesting work

- Promotion and growth in the organization

- Personal loyalty to employees

- Good working conditions

- Tactful discipline

Now go back over the list and identify the order you think your employees would choose.

Over the past fifty years, several studies have been conducted in which employees were asked to rank these ten rewards in terms of their importance or motivational value to them. Then the supervisors of these employees were asked to rank the same items according to how they thought their employees would rank them. The first study was conducted in 1946, the second in 1981, and the most recent in 1995. In all three cases, the results show that what managers and supervisors thought was important to employees is different from what employees say. In all three studies, employees ranked job security and good wages near the middle, yet supervisors believed their employees would put good wages and job security in slots one and two, respectively. In fact, in the 1995 study conducted by Kenneth Kovack at George Mason University, supervisor and employee ranking looks like this:

	Supervisor	Employee
• Full appreciation of work done	8	2
• Feeling of being in on things	10	3
• Help on personal problems	9	10
• Job security	2	4
• Good wages	1	5
• Interesting work	5	1
• Promotion and growth	3	6
• Loyalty from boss	6	8
• Working conditions	4	7
• Tactful disciplining	7	9

From "Employee Motivation: Addressing a Crucial Factor in Your Organization's Performance" by Dr. Kenneth A. Kovach. Reprinted with permission.

Notice that supervisors put *feeling of being in on things* as number ten, and employees rank it among the top three. These studies show that managers are often totally wrong in predicting how their employees would rank the list. What's the impact? Simply put, if managers misinterpret what is important to their employees, they will choose methods of motivation that are entirely off base. For example, a manager may believe that all employees are motivated primarily by money. So the manager gives everyone a bonus. Much to his or her surprise, employee performance does not improve. What the manager does not realize is that there may be other factors that are more important to the employees.

So how do you find out what motivates your employees? Well, you could ask them to complete the above assessment as a start, although you may not get accurate data. The best way is to talk to your employees and really listen to them. They will let you know indirectly or sometimes even directly what's important to them. For example, if you have an employee who frequently asks you, "How am I doing?" or "Did you like the way I handled that situation?" that's a good indication that particular employee wants and needs recognition.

Identifying the Manager's Role

At this point, you might be asking yourself, "What is my role as a leader in the motivation process?" Your responsibility in motivating employees is to create the environment that promotes motivation within the individual. Therefore, you must first understand employees' needs and then show them the benefits of moving them from where they are to where you want them to be. In other words, point out the W.I.I.F.T. - What's In It For Them. People have reasons for everything they do. People are motivated to do what they do based on personal reasons and benefits. The "what's in it for me" (WIIFM) is a primary mover of people. If we are to be successful at influencing others, we need to identify the other person's WIIFM.

Understanding Today's Employees

Times have changed and so have employees. What worked ten or fifteen years ago is not appropriate for today's employees. Motivating employees is complicated further by generational differences. More than ever before, today's managers are finding themselves managing people their own age, older, or younger. And the key to getting the most from each group differs considerably. For example, my age group (born roughly between 1943 and 1960) was influenced greatly by the events of the '60s and '70s, including the Vietnam War, race riots, the woman's movement, and television. Idealistic and moralistic, the baby boomers' primary motivators have been money and freedom. Our parents (born 1920 to 1942) were impacted by the Great Depression and believe strongly in the importance of security and loyalty. Strongly adhering to tradition and what their parents said, they have been motivated by status and security. Finally, we have the so-called "Generation X" (born during the years 1961 to 1979), who have grown up on computers, video games, and VCRs and who are both realistic and cynical. They have grown up watching their "workaholic" parents spend fourteen to sixteen hours at the office, foregoing family vacations, only to find themselves tossed out after twenty-five years of loyal service to the company. Generation X says, "That's not for me." Unwilling to pay their dues, they want what they want now and if they don't get it, they're "outta here," moving on to greener pastures. Forget loyalty. They're interested in rewarding challenges and are willing to work hard, yet unlike their parents, fiercely guard their personal and leisure time. Because many grew up in dual career or single-parent families, they are self-reliant and independent and are not as intimidated by authority figures as those in previous generations.

In order to be effective in creating a positive motivational climate, we need to take a look at what characterizes today's employees. The following points are characteristic of contemporary employees, regardless of age:

- They see compensation as a consequence of performance and therefore expect to be rewarded accordingly.

- They are more concerned with organizational recognition.

- They have more desire to participate in decisions that affect them.

- They value communication from management and the opportunity to communicate to management.

- They tend to have a short-term goal orientation.

- They want work to be challenging, interesting, and creative.

- They desire developmental opportunities.

- They tend to place their priorities first with leisure, then family, and finally work.

Take a moment and think about the implication of these characteristics on the workplace and your responsibility to motivate.

Research shows that employee motivation falls into two categories: maintainers and motivators. Maintainers are factors that must be kept at a satisfactory level and include the following:

- working conditions
- company policies
- job security
- pay and benefits
- relationships
- supervision
- status

The following are true motivators, that is, factors that create an inner desire to work by satisfying certain needs that are important to the individual:

- achievement
- recognition
- job itself
- responsibility
- advancement
- growth

As a manager, analyze your organization based on these two categories. Does it measure up? If not, what can you do to improve the situation and create a positive motivational climate?

Empowerment Mindset

For empowerment to work, everyone in the collective unit - corporation, community, or family - must adopt and develop a self-management mindset. They must view relationships as collaborative and interdependent where people are comfortable both giving and receiving feedback. Furthermore, the structure, policies, procedures, and systems must support an empowerment culture.

To be a successful influencer/motivator, you must first understand that you cannot motivate anyone. You can only create an environment that encourages and promotes the person's self-motivation. Someone once said that motivation is getting people to do what you want them to do because THEY WANT to do it. The challenge - whether you are a manager or a parent - is to give others a reason to want to do what you want them to do because doing it will satisfy a need they have. You have to tune into their needs, not yours.

You must also keep in mind that you are the critical component in the motivation process. Your actions set the tone. Many people in power positions are still using some old-fashioned and ineffective methods of motivating people. Some people embrace the "carrot-on-the-stick" approach. These practices take the form of incentive programs, promises of rewards, and bonuses. Others employ the symbolic "whip" or "club" by emphasizing the negative results of their behavior. For example, a manager might say, "If you don't start getting to work on time, you'll be fired" or "You'll never get ahead if you continue to make these kinds of mistakes." A parent might tell his child to behave or she'll "be grounded for three months." The problem with these methods is that they are short-term. These "quick fixes" create no permanent behavior change.

The next time instead of a whip, you will probably have to use a "club" or the carrot you've been dangling in front of someone will have to be bigger. On the other hand, think about a flowering plant as a metaphor for getting the best from others. In order to get that plant to bloom, you must create the appropriate environment using the right amount of light, water, temperature, and fertilizer. And if you have different types of plants, each will require different care. People are no different. Each person requires a different approach. It is crucial for managers to understand what drives their employees. The key is to identify what it is that each person wants and figure out in what environments different people thrive.

Do you really encourage people and bring out the best in them or do you manage them through intimidation and threats? What motivation methods have you tried? Did they work? If so, for how long?

Your Empowerment Profile

To test your own empowerment proficiency, ask yourself the following questions:

Do I...

- Encourage my employees to take risks?
- Model the behavior I expect of others?
- Encourage people to take responsibility for their own actions?
- Create a climate of openness and trust?
- Value diversity of style and behavior?
- Involve others in decisions?
- Share rewards and recognition?
- Communicate expectations?
- Help people work together?
- Showcase others' accomplishments?

If you were not able to answer "yes" to each of these questions, take a look at your current interpersonal practices and identify influencing behaviors you want to modify or adopt.

Creating the Environment

Since personal power already exists in each individual, empowerment is not something someone can give to another. The only way to release that personal internal power is to remove the barriers that prevent its expression and create an environment in which people are motivated to do a good job.

Provide Adequate Training

As mentioned earlier, we need to give people the skills they need to do their jobs. They also need training in interpersonal skills such as conflict resolution, listening, decision making, problem solving, process improvement, and communication.

Use Appropriate Reinforcement

We should reinforce those behaviors that we want repeated; therefore, rewards should be tied to specific performance. If you have determined that delivering quality service is important, then the employee's performance in delivering that service should be rewarded. For example, the employee who "goes the extra mile" by personally delivering an item to a customer who is ill and cannot get to your place of business should be acknowledged and rewarded accordingly.

Keep in mind, however, that reinforcement is personal. What reinforces one person may not reinforce another. Most parents of more than one child recognize that what one child values, another finds absolutely meaningless. One child may prefer being rewarded with something tangible such as a small gift or a special meal prepared just for him. His or her sibling, on the other hand, would rather be excused from doing a particular chore.

The same is true of employees. Some employees prefer to be rewarded with time off; others with a gift or plaque; still others might be happy with public recognition at a staff meeting or their name mentioned in the company newsletter.

Think of a recent incident when one of your employees went above and beyond the call of duty. Did you reward him or her in some way? If not, what could you have done to reinforce the behavior you want repeated?

It is also important to dispense reinforcement as soon as possible after the desired performance.

Give People Choices

Whenever possible, give people a chance to make a decision. Choice and the personal commitment that results are essential to motivation. People who are not given the opportunity to choose for themselves tend to become passive and lethargic. Although they may perform tasks and even meet expectations, they do so without that spark of enthusiasm and excitement that brings meaning to what they do. People want and need to be involved in decisions that affect them. For example, if you are thinking about remodeling or redesigning the employee work area, give the employees the guidelines and parameters, then allow them to design the area themselves.

Provide Support

One key characteristic of the achievement-oriented person is the willingness to use help when it is needed. People should be encouraged to ask for support and assistance; otherwise, they will become frustrated. Asking for help should never be considered a sign of weakness; it should be considered a sign of strength.

When an employee comes to you for help, be careful not to turn him or her off with comments such as "You still don't know how to do that? I thought I explained it to you." Instead, ask, "Tell me where you are having problems. What can I clear up for you?"

Offer Encouragement

A powerful influencing skill is the ability to offer encouragement. We can develop a sense of competence and confidence in others by encouraging them to take risks, acknowledge their own accomplishments, and strive to achieve their personal best.

Point out improvements in performance, no matter how small. This is particularly important when employees, for example, are beginning work on new tasks or when your child is learning a new skill. In getting others to improve performance, frequent encouragement can be useful; however, it should be reduced as the person becomes more confident and proficient.

As Goethe once said, "Correction does much, but encouragement does more; encouragement after censure is as the sun after a shower."

Communicate the Big Picture

Routine work can result in passivity and boredom unless employees are aware of how the routine tasks contribute to their own development and the success of the organization. Taking the time to explain how what they do fits into the "big picture" can increase commitment and productivity tremendously.

Think about a task one of your employees does routinely. Outline a plan to explain how this task ties into organizational goals.

Match Tasks and Environments to People's Needs

What may satisfy one person may not satisfy another. The observant manager is aware of the more basic needs of the employee such as affiliation, approval, and achievement. Remember the study of what people want from their jobs?

Refer to the list of motivators. Choose two employees and try to determine what motivates each of them. Then identify what you can do to meet each person's individual need.

Listen Carefully to Complaints

It is important to handle problems and complaints before they get blown out of proportion. People feel more significant when their complaints are taken seriously. Conversely, nothing hurts as much as when others view a personally significant problem as unimportant. By telling someone, "It's no big deal" or "You shouldn't feel that way" you devalue the individual. You may not think it's important, but it is to the employee. Acknowledge the complaint and its validity, then solicit the employee's input in resolving it.

Criticize Behavior Not People

Although we discussed the concept of focusing on specific behavior in Strategy #3 on feedback, it bears repeating. Always remember to respect the individual. A person can do a task poorly and still be a valuable employee. Too many people are inappropriately labeled "dumb," "incompetent," "lazy," or "unqualified."

Be sure to address behavior, not attitude. Managers often have difficulty distinguishing between attitude and behavior. Take, for example, the following statement: "Janet does not take her work seriously." Is that an attitude or behavior statement? The answer is attitude. An attitude is a conclusion which identifies a feeling or emotion about an observed situation. A behavior, on the other hand, is something that can be observed. To state the above example in terms of behavior, you might write, "Janet's reports contain errors that require rewriting. She misses deadlines that affect the timeliness of our quarterly statements."

How might you rewrite the following statements?
- Leslie is incompetent.
- Vince is sloppy in his work.
- Tom shows lack of interest in his job.
- Joan is rude to customers.

Encourage Employees to Set Their Own Goals and Objectives

Let employees participate actively in the goal-setting process. People tend to know their own capabilities and limitations. Also, personal goal setting results in a commitment to goal accomplishment. In setting sales goals, for example, ask your sales person to come up with a realistic monthly goal and a plan to reach that number. Then the two of you should sit down and evaluate the goal by applying the following criteria:

- Is the goal specific? Write the goal so that anyone would be able to identify exactly what you are going to accomplish.

- Is it measurable? Identify the deliverable.

- Is it agreed upon? All those involved must agree. In most cases, this means the manager and the employee who makes it happen.

- Is it realistic? Make sure that you have the appropriate resources (time, skills, equipment, environment, money) to successfully meet the goal.

- Is it timebound? Set deadlines, interim reviews, and target completion dates.

Think of an employee you would like to involve in the goal-setting process. Then outline how you are going to approach him or her. What will you say to communicate the reasons you are asking the employee to set his or her own goals? Are there any guidelines or parameters he or she should consider?

Clarify Your Expectations

Make sure that employees understand your expectations. Regardless of the size of your organization, you should have a job description for every position, clearly outlining qualifications and responsibilities. Also identify the expected standards of performance. For example, if you expect the telephone to be answered within three rings, say so. Employees are not mind readers. You cannot assume that just because they have experience in doing the job, they know what you specifically expect of them in that position.

Identify a position in your organization and write a job description for it. If you already have written job descriptions, choose one and review it to make sure it is clear and includes specific standards of performance.

Have a Flexible Management Style

Many managers pride themselves on treating everyone the same. This practice can be dangerous. Employees are individuals with individual needs. You need to treat everyone fairly but not necessarily the same. A flexible management style also means that you vary your approach not only with each individual but also with each situation. An employee who is new to the job will need more direction than a five-year veteran. However, if the veteran employee is given a new task or responsibility, that person may need more direction in that particular situation.

How would you characterize your management style? Do you use the same approach in every situation? Think about situations or people that would require you to modify your style accordingly.

Provide Immediate and Relevant Feedback

Give feedback that will help employees improve their performance in the future. Feedback is most effective when it follows performance. Feedback should be relevant to the task and should provide employees with information on how they might improve their performance at the task. Never give negative feedback without providing informational feedback. Keep in mind that feedback should be both positive and negative. Employees often complain that the only time they receive feedback is when they do something wrong. Practice catching people doing something right and tell them about it. The feedback also must be specific. Just telling someone that they're doing a good job and "keep up the good work" is of no help. It is much more effective and meaningful to say something like, "John, I liked the way you handled that difficult customer. You showed a great deal of restraint and professionalism by not raising your voice or losing control."

Identify a recent event in which an employee did something outstanding. What, if anything, did you say about the employee's performance? Would you say it differently now?

Eliminate Barriers to Individual Achievement

Many people who are labeled "failures" or "incompetents" are simply being hindered by relatively minor obstacles that managers have not recognized. The tragedy is that after a while, the employee may begin to accept the failure label as a fact. Does the employee have the knowledge and skills to do the job? If not, it's your job to provide him or her with the necessary training. Does the person have the appropriate tools or technology? If not, get it. Make sure people have the training, information, tools, and equipment to do the job.

Identify an employee who does not seem to be as motivated as you would like. Ask yourself if there is a barrier that perhaps you have not previously considered. Then plan how you might check out your theory.

Exhibit Confidence in Employees

There is a great deal of research to support the contention that people who are expected to achieve will do so more frequently than others. Saying to the employee, "I know this new procedure may be uncomfortable and maybe even difficult for you at first, but I know you will be able to make the adjustment" is more effective than "Give it a try. If you can't get the hang of it, we'll have to see what we can do." The latter statement has conveyed the subtle message that you expect the person to fail.

As we discussed earlier in Strategy #6: Expectation, the concept of the self-fulfilling prophecy or Pygmalion Effect is very powerful. Positive Pygmalions encourage employees to ask questions; they allow more time to do a job correctly; and they give employees the benefit of the doubt.

What can you do to demonstrate confidence in your employees?

Establish a Climate of Trust and Open Communication

Productivity is highest in organizations that encourage openness and trust. Trust and openness are created by the way we communicate. Do you use phrases that build people and get things started or ones that destroy ideas and chloroform creative thinking? Think about the "discourager" and "encourager" phrases in Strategy #8. Which do you use more frequently?

Be careful not to give mixed messages. People receive mixed messages when the verbal and nonverbal actions are not communicating the same message. The manager who says, "I'm listening" and continues to look through papers on his or her desk is communicating that he or she really isn't interested in what the employee has to say.

Think about a recent employee complaint that you regarded as trivial. How did you respond to the employee? Is there anything you would have done or said differently?

Be a Role Model

Demonstrate your own motivation through behavior and attitude. Nothing turns people off faster than a manager who doesn't practice what he or she preaches. Be a role model. If you expect people to be on time, then you must make sure you are on time, too. If you expect employees to treat customers with courtesy and respect, you should treat employees the same way. If you expect employees to get additional training to upgrade their knowledge and skills, you should be attending workshops and seminars to fine-tune your management skills as well.

Think about any areas where you might not be modeling the appropriate behavior. What can you do differently?

Ensuring Success

At first, those you wish to empower may be reluctant to take on additional responsibilities. Those who have never been given the opportunity to participate in decisions or to use their own judgment may be suspicious and may just need a little reassurance that you really are on the level. In other cases, they may need additional training or coaching in particular skills, such as decision making or problem solving. Managers, for example, will need to help people get in touch with their personal power and help them develop the competencies they need to handle the additional power, responsibility, and authority. People in workplace environments that are experiencing downsizing may be afraid to take risks because they are fearful that their jobs may be at stake. Once again, the manager is the key force to help them overcome their fears and encourage commitment, risk-taking, and innovation.

Mastering the Art of Influencing

Throughout this book we have explored strategies and skills you can use to improve your effectiveness in influencing others. Mastering the art of influencing takes time, practice, and a willingness to try new behaviors and modify old ones. Each situation and interaction is different, requiring you to select the appropriate "mix" from your personal "palette" of interpersonal skills. By applying some of the techniques discussed in this book, you will become more effective in both your personal and professional relationships and will truly become a master of _The Art of Influencing_.